WILDERNESS
SURVIVAL
GUIDE

WILDERNESS
SURVIVAL
GUIDE

365 TIPS FOR STAYING ALIVE
IN THE WOODS

DAVE CANTERBURY

New York

FALL RIVER PRESS

New York

An Imprint of Sterling Publishing Co., Inc.
1166 Avenue of the Americas
New York, NY 10036

ISBN 978-1-4351-6557-1

For information about custom editions, special sales, and premium and
corporate purchases, please contact Sterling Special Sales at 800-805-5489
or specialsales@sterlingpublishing.com.

Manufactured in China

2 4 6 8 10 9 7 5 3

www.sterlingpublishing.com

"The doctorate in woodsy knowledge can only be taught by Mother Nature in the classroom of the outdoors. Many can train you but only experience can teach you."

—DAVE CANTERBURY

PLAN THE SCOPE
OF YOUR TRIP

Short-term trips in the woods are great opportunities to practice skills and take chances with a smaller kit. Traveling with fewer implements requires a lot of improvisation. On a short jaunt, it does not matter much if your shelter is uncomfortable or if your trapping campaign is not overly successful. Use short-term trips as opportunities for learning and know that if something does not turn out quite right, you can practice again next time to make it better.

Five Cs of Survivability

1. CUTTING TOOLS: knives, axes, saws

2. COMBUSTION DEVICES: ferrocerium rod, lighter, magnifying lens

3. COVER ELEMENTS: seasonal clothing with outerwear, tarps, wool blankets, sleeping bag, emergency bivvy, hammock, small tent

4. CONTAINERS: water bottles, canteens, nesting cook pots and pans

5. CORDAGE: bank line, paracord, rope, webbing, mule tape

Five More Cs of Survivability

1. COTTON MATERIALS: bandannas, shemagh, netting, cloth shards

2. CARGO TAPE: duct tape

3. CANDLING DEVICES: headlamps, candles, crank lights

4. COMPASSES: your preferred brand along with a small backup like a quality button-style

5. CANVAS REPAIR NEEDLE: wedge-style needle for repairing heavy materials

Clothing

Pack at least two full sets of socks and undergarments, trousers, and shirts. Carry clothing that is comfortable in all seasons or be prepared to pack enough clothing for two different climates (for a total of four sets). Take 10–12-ounce durable canvas pants like the tree-climbing pants offered by Arborwear. Long-sleeved, lightweight, canvas, button-down shirts are comfortable in all seasons, and cotton T-shirts take advantage of evaporative cooling in the summer.

Winter Clothing

In winter, use a heavy wool layer that will act as insulation, such as the merino wool pants offered by Minus33. In general, nothing beats wool in cold-weather climates. It is comfortable, fire retardant, repels moisture, and even when it is wet it still acts as a good insulation. If freezing rain and sleet are an issue, combine the wool with an oilcloth raincoat.

Headgear

Never underestimate the importance of hats when planning your kit. A good hat will protect you from the sun and conserve body heat—most of which is released through the head and the neck. A felted wide-brim hat works well in spring, summer, and fall. A wool beanie or toboggan will help combat the cold in winter. In the most severe weather, old leather bomber caps with earflaps and fur linings are very comfortable.

Footwear

Leather boots are an absolute must for long-term wilderness activities. When choosing your footwear, remember that boots are only as waterproof as they are high. Carrying a second pair of boots will save a lot of trouble on long-term trips so you can alternate and avoid wearing them out too quickly. Bring a pair of moccasins to wear when walking around camp so that you give your boots an occasional rest. Moccasins, elk hide or buffalo, are also handy when stalking game in dry leaves.

Round Your Neck

Kerchiefs and scarves have been staples of the woodsman's kit
for hundreds of years. Their uses go well beyond the obvious.
The cotton netting used as a sniper veil works very well in summer
and makes a great improvised net for fishing. Kerchiefs made from
cotton, like the shemagh, are effective across three seasons. In winter,
a 4' × 4' scarf not only keeps you warm but can also be used as a
cape to repel snow.

Gloves and Mittens

A sturdy pair of leather calfskin gloves will protect the hands
from briars, brambles, and blisters when doing normal camp chores.
In winter, arctic mittens with wool glove liners are indispensable.
To stay comfortable for a full day on the trail or trapline, keeping
your extremities warm is just as important as conserving heat on
your core.

FARMED

Remember this acronym when purchasing tools for your kit. It is especially helpful when you are trying to choose between multiple brands and styles.

- FUNCTIONALITY—Is this tool designed for only one specific purpose?

- AFFORDABILITY—Does this tool fit into my budget?

- REPEATABILITY—Can I perform tasks the same way with this tool and get the same result each time?

- MAINTAINABILITY—Is this tool easy to maintain over time?

- ERGONOMICS—Does this tool feel good to me for my body stature and build?

- DURABILITY—Is the tool of good quality that will last for years if well maintained?

Checklist of Five Most Important Tools

These tools should be the basis of your kit. When deciding which versions of these tools to include in your kit, think about the environmental factors, the type of shelter you plan to build, and the length of your stay.

- Knife
- Axe
- Saw
- Carving tool
- Awl

Three Knives Worth Carrying

- 5"–6" knife for butchering
- Knife for fine carving
- Folding knife of high-carbon steel, which can be kept in your pocket

Knife Profiles

A knife with a butchering profile is best for processing game meat. A slender blade width is better for fine carving tasks, boning, and filleting. Processing game for food, tools, and hides is more critical than carving notches, so you will need a blade that is specific to this task. A knife for food processing should be about 4"–5" long and fairly thin at about 1/8" or less. A Scandinavian (V) grind will be most useful, but a flat grind is a close second. Both are easily maintained in the field but are strong enough to act as a primary blade should you need a replacement.

JACK KNIFE

CLIP POINT KNIFE

TRAILING POINT KNIFE

SHEATH KNIFE

MACHETE

Sheath Knives

Many argue a sheath knife should be enough to accomplish tasks from fine carving and processing game to splitting firewood. Even if you lose your pack, this knife will always be on your person. Keeping this in mind, be sure to practice using your knife for various tasks before embarking on a long journey.

Carving Tools

In the eastern woodlands, the jackknife, or folding knife, has been considered the best for whittling or fine carving. Morakniv carries a fine line of carving tools. The crooked knife, or mocotaugan, was a standard carry tool for many native peoples. This knife, similar to the bent knife by Deepwoods Ventures, can be used for tasks as versatile as carving canoe paddles to manufacturing replacement handles.

Fleshing Knives

Fleshing knives work well for removing the flesh from a large hide. These knives have a dull, hard edge and are available commercially, or you can use a split bone from the animal itself.

"The clearest way into the Universe is through a forest wilderness."

—JOHN MUIR

Point Blankets

Point blankets have a series of colored lines (points) woven into them on one edge signifying the size of the blanket. Modern point blankets can be found up to six points, or approximately 96" × 96". In today's terms, a four-point blanket would fit a full-sized bed, and a six-point blanket would fit a queen- or king-sized bed. In the old days, these points were also used to signify how many finished or "made" beaver hides the blanket was worth. So a six-point blanket was worth the value of six "made" beavers or the equivalent in another fur.

Birch Tar

Birch oil can be rendered into birch tar. To create birch tar, slowly heat the oil to a boil like a gravy and then stir. Be careful, because both the fumes and the liquid are highly flammable. Once rendered to a thick paste you can roll it onto a stick where it can be stored for later use. This form of storage is called a pitch stick. Birch tar, when reheated, is a completely waterproof gluing material. It is also a flexible adhesive and can be used for hafting and sealing both containers and leathers such as moccasin seams.

Char Material

There are many advantages to making char material. For one, char is highly combustible, so adding it to the marginal materials within a bird's nest gives an extended heat source for effecting ignition. In fact, char material can be ignited with almost any spark from old lighters, ferrocerium rods, or a sunglass. Given its variety of ignition methods, char is an important material to keep a good supply of in your kit.

Igniting Materials

Most softwood species can be scraped with the back of the knife to create fine shavings for ignition with an open flame or a ferrocerium rod. Inner barks and barks of things like cedar, poplar, grape vine (water vine), and honeysuckle will make a combustible nest if dry.

Fatwood

Fatwood is the woodsman's sure fire, and it works well even in the dampest conditions. Fine scrapings and shavings of resinous fatwood pine will ignite easily and burn long enough to catch marginal tinder sources.

Birch Bark Fire Starter

Birch bark, which contains a volatile oil, will also be highly flammable with an open flame but can be processed to increase the surface area for use with a ferrocerium rod as well. An old Sami method of making fire is to roll tinder in a birch bark tube and then place an ember in the back of this tube closest to the mouth and gently blow. This protects the ember while allowing heat to rise through the tinder and the birch bark. It also adds fuel for longevity once the fire is ignited.

Caves As Shelters

Before using a cave as a permanent shelter dwelling, inspect it.
Look for animal feces, bones, and smells of urine. Falling rock
can also present a danger, so make a visual inspection with a
good light source of the ceiling and walls. Look for fissures or
cracks in the stone that might be compounded by heat from a
fire. Consider the height of the ceiling. The lower the ceiling
height of the cave, the more a fire will affect the structure's
integrity. Caves with higher ceilings will also provide much
better ventilation.

Bricks

To make bricks you can use cement and shape it with a form
made from wood. It will take several of these forms to make
many bricks at a time. Pack the materials into the brick form
and use a split stick as a scraper to level the top. Let the bricks
dry in the sun for several days and they will shrink a little bit,
making it very easy to remove them from the mold. You can
also make fired bricks similar to the way you make clay pots,
but the binder material used must be more selective, such as
cattail fluff or crushed shells.

Deadfall Traps

Deadfalling traps are not always intended to instantly kill prey; some of the smaller deadfalls used for microtrapping rodent species will suffocate the animal instead. Many people raise a deadfall such as a rock or log at a high angle, thinking this will help them achieve crushing power and kill quickly. The truth is, the higher the angle of the deadfall, the greater the chance the animal will escape the trap before the object makes contact.

Live Animals

One of the main concepts to keep in mind for long-term wilderness living is that live food never spoils. The important thing to remember is that you should not process the food straight away, only care for it while you have it alive. This can be of big advantage in hot weather, but it can also be troublesome if you are in an area with many large predatory animals. This principle is very advantageous when you've caught animals such as turtles and frogs, which can be kept for a time in a sack or bag.

"To poke a wood fire is more solid enjoyment than almost anything else in the world."

—CHARLES DUDLEY WARNER

Acorn Tannins

The tannins that give acorns their astringent taste can be a great resource for other things like medicines and tanning. Save the liquid from the first boiling pot of water you used to leech the acorn meat and reserve it for later use. Astringents work best for external use in a wash or poultice, and the solution will be antiparasitic as well.

Charcoal

If you don't have access to coal, you can create charcoal from hardwoods used for forging exactly the same way you make any other char materials. To do this, you will need a large container as well as a very large and long-burning fire. An alternative is to use normal hardwood in a fire pit and build a large coal bed. If you have forced air, a slit trench–type fire works well here. You can also make a trench above ground with large piles of sand, dirt, or rocks on each side to hold heat better from thermal mass.

Forge Welding—Step One

Before attempting this weld you will need to clean the surfaces to be welded with a wire brush—while they are orange-hot, if possible. Then add sand for a flux before the final heat to weld. Now get the metal almost white-hot. It will appear very bright yellow, and a few sparks should be coming from it. Be careful, because if you wait a few seconds too long, you will melt off the work in the forge and all will be lost.

Forge Welding—Step Two

Once the welding heat is attained it is critical to get the piece or pieces to the anvil and strike several times. Don't smash the metal with heavy blows; just pound hard enough to compress it when in this near-liquid state. It may require a few more orange/yellow heats to complete the process, but to be effective, a good weld should happen on the first time.

Useful Items from the Forge

- Nails
- Log dogs
- Froe
- Auger
- Raft dog
- Squirrel cooker
- Fire irons

- Hooks
- Hold fasts
- Adze
- Wood chisels
- Mortise chisels
- Brace

Blacksmithing

In the old days, the blacksmith was like an engineer. He needed to make precise tools that would aid every member of society from the farmer to the doctor to the hunter and trapper. The ability to manipulate metal has always been a mainstay of survivability.

Burn Container

To make a burn container, start a fire on a flat wood surface. Control the circular burn to drive deeper into the material by alternating between burning and scraping the raw material, burning and scraping again, and shaping it into a container.

Coil Pots

Start with a flat round of clay similar to a pancake. Roll a long tube out of the rest of the clay and then wrap it around the base as coils, stacking them until you reach the desired height. Smooth the inside of the pot using some water on your fingers.

Pinch Pots

To make a pinch pot, start with a ball of clay that is suitable for the size pot you need to make. Place your thumbs into the center and progressively pinch the clay all around, pinching and pulling the clay between your thumb and fingers. Keep pinching and pulling outward from the center, forming the pot until it reaches the desired size.

The Moon Method

You can use the phases of the moon, outside of the new and full moon, to determine direction pretty easily. Observe any crescent moon and trace a line from tip to tip and then to the horizon. That will give you a southerly direction.

Watch As Direction Finder

Your watch can be a direction finder even if it has no hands. If you have a watch, point the hour hand toward the sun and halfway between the hour hand and 12 will be southerly. If you have a digital watch, just draw a watch face with hands on paper to match the one on your wrist.

Finding South

Moss does not always grow on the north side of the tree, but the heaviest vegetation will always point southerly to take advantage of photosynthesis.

Growth Rings

If you cut down a tree, the growth rings can help with direction finding; the tighter rings will be wider on the southern side.

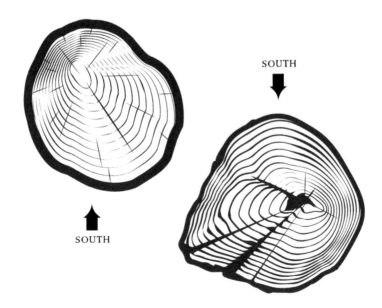

SOUTH

SOUTH

Axe

Your main axe should be at least 18"–20" in handle length. A larger axe of 26"–28" in handle length will be much more effective for big tasks such as cutting down large trees. Aside from handle configurations, there are also many head designs and profiles available. An axe with a head weight of up to 3 pounds is good for felling. When selecting an axe, most of the right dimensions come down to personal preference.

Tomahawks

The tomahawk, a personal tool that hangs on the belt, is a backup to a knife. One of the handiest things about the tomahawk is that the handle can be removed so you can use the head alone as a scraping or skinning tool. Tomahawks are too small to process large amounts of firewood or fell large trees, but their handles can be replaced fairly easily if broken, which makes them a good choice for long excursions. There are a lot of tomahawks on the market today, but the ones with heavier heads are most advantageous for wood-processing tasks.

Hatchets

The decision to carry a tomahawk or a hatchet depends on your individual needs and the environment. A smaller crafting-type hatchet can be carried along with the larger axe. Hatchets can be carried right on the belt and are very easy to wield with one hand. They are handy for fine carving and small chopping when processing fire materials. Look for varieties that are designed to put the center-line blade in the proper location when you are choking up on the handle so that it works as a carving or skinning tool as well.

Saws

Folding saws make an excellent addition to your kit as long as the blade is not one with larger teeth and a wider kerf, or distance between teeth; these do not make fine cuts. It is better to select something with smaller teeth and a narrow kerf. A folding saw is most efficient when it doubles as a notch-cutting saw, and for that reason, a crosscutting blade will be much easier to control and your cuts will be cleaner.

FOLDING SAW

Fixed-Blade Saws

These saws include not only crosscutting or dovetail saws but also pruning blades. The type of saws you include in your kit will be dictated by what you plan to do with them. If you are carrying a bucksaw or bow saw that has a green-wood blade, then a simple crosscut blade with a bit finer teeth will be much more desirable than a pruning-type, green-wood blade.

CROSSCUT SAWS

Bow Saws and Bucksaws (Frame Saws)

Include one of these in any winter kit, no matter the length of your stay. For longer-term kits, just be sure that the blade is at least 20" long and has both a green-wood and dry- wood blade. The advantage to a bow (metal-frame saw) is durability. It is useful for long-term outings. Even though it is made from metal, the frame is actually a hollow tube so the difference in weight is negligible.

Awl

Awls are designed to punch holes in materials such as leather, bark, and wood. There are many different types of awls, but the crooked awl is the most versatile. These tools are two-sided with three or four sides to each point. The taper of the awl is usually a little different on opposing ends so that you have some versatility when drilling holes. You can easily fashion a handle for one end of this tool if needed or add a hole for lockstitch sewing tasks.

Temporary Shelters

Even if you are planning to set up a permanent shelter, you need to be prepared to set up a temporary shelter in case you need to leave base camp for a day or two. A good Egyptian cotton, oilcloth tarp of 8' × 8' minimum, like the one available from Tentsmiths, combined with a moisture barrier such as a tick mattress and a stout woolen blanket, will do in the coldest of climates. Just make sure you have a proper bed and fire.

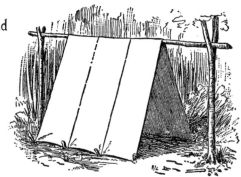

Hammocks

Hammocks can be a great three-season option when combined with a blanket. They can even be used in cold weather if you use some kind of quality underquilt that will combat convection issues associated with hanging above ground. A lot of hammock manufacturers now make a bug net that is either built into the hammock or available as an add-on. These nets create a screened enclosure, offering added protection from bugs.

Tents

Small backpacking-style tents provide comfort and security from bugs and other wigglers. However, they restrict your view and eliminate fire as a heat source. Select the tent that is made of the heaviest material you feel comfortable carrying. You will appreciate the durability. One other possible downside to consider is that condensation tends to form inside the tent walls at night, which can make them colder than open shelter. Look for varieties with mesh tops and a rain flap, which helps alleviate the condensation issues.

"Preconceived notions, especially when one is fairly brought up in their influence, are most difficult to shake off."

—STEWART EDWARD WHITE, *CAMP AND TRAIL*

Bivvies

A bivvy is usually a small tube-style bag that is made for a single person and can be set up very quickly. The same rules apply to bivvies as to tents: Look for durable material with mesh and a closable rain flap to help prevent condensation. Some manufacturers offer bivvies that have a sleeping bag included, like a self-contained sleeping unit.

Ultralight Cots

Ultralight cots provide a comfortable raised bed in just a couple of minutes. These cots fold up very small and are extremely light, which makes them a great option for a good night's sleep on longer treks.

Tent Cots

Tent cots are made especially for hunting. These are self-contained tents and sleeping cots built into one unit. They can be quite comfortable and provide all the advantages of a raised bed and closed tent.

Prioritizing Items of Convenience

- Repair kits with additional tools

- Premade tinders and fire extenders

- Varied cookware such as folding reflector ovens and skillets

- Additional tarps for making shelter over work areas

- Additional cordage for major projects like nets

Most Precious Goes Last

Save the most precious resources as a last option. For example, never start a fire with a lighter if you can use a ferro rod, and never use a ferro rod if you can use the sun (which is a renewable resource).

Think Like a Possum

"Opossum mentality" is always key: Think like a scavenger. Never pass over a needed resource thinking that you will run into it again. This is especially true with materials related to fire, food, or medicine.

Pinewood As Fuel

Pinewood is fantastic because, due to its resinous nature, it will burn quickly and can be used to make a fire lay even in wet weather. The dark black smoke that you see from a fire made with pine is a product of the resins from within the wood burning off. Pine is a softwood that can make a very effective bow-drill hearth and spindle set—although be careful to avoid the resins or the set will simply polish and not burn. Pine makes a decent carving wood but is not as durable for utensils as other woods.

Pine Resin

Pine resin is usually found on the outermost part of the tree where an injury has occurred. The dripping or secretion allows you to access and collect something from inside the tree without hurting it. This resin, or sap, is like liquid gold and should be collected at any opportunity that presents itself. As a medicinal resource, pine sap can act like new skin on a shallow cut and generally works as an antiseptic when caring for wounds.

Pine Pitch

Pine resin itself is highly flammable and is therefore a great flame extender within the fire lay. A very good adhesive, called pine pitch, can be made by heating the sap and adding equal parts charcoal and a binder like cattail fluff or herbivore dung. Use a low heat when melting the sap because it becomes very brittle when burned. Store the resulting glue in a tin or wrap it on a pitch stick by winding it on a stick and drying it one layer at a time. Heat this stick over a fire to soften the glue for application.

Pine Needles

Needles on eastern pines are extremely nutritious and have more vitamin C per weight than a fresh-squeezed orange. Also high in vitamin A, these pine needles make an excellent tea for boosting the immune system. Pine needle tea also works as an expectorant and a decongestant. The tea can even be used as an antiseptic wash or fomentation. Not all pines taste the same, so you should try different types to find what you like best.

Pine Needle Baskets

You can fashion beautiful coil baskets from pine needles, although this task is tedious. Dead pine needles are fantastic additions to any fire lay as the resinous needles are highly flammable. They also make good coarse materials for a bird's nest when making primitive fire.

Pine Roots

Certain tree species, such as the spruce, have very long roots that grow just under the surface of the ground. Harvest these roots in long lengths and use them for cord or basket weaving. Once the root is harvested, the outer bark must be removed to make the root more pliable. You can remove the bark by pinching the root between two sticks and pulling the root through, removing the bark as you go. Keep the roots wet so that they are easier to handle. Larger roots can be further split to make the resource last even longer.

Fatwood

The area of the tree commonly known as the fatwood will collect the resins best because it's where the sap settles. Oftentimes the stump and root ball can be an excellent source of fatwood. Not all tree species have a lot of sap, so you will need to experiment with what you have. It is safe to say that all pines will contain some fatwood. Many times, a dead standing or fallen tree will have a root ball that is completely saturated with resin. If you find yourself in need of an emergency fire-starting device, remember that fatwood is highly flammable.

Harvesting Fatwood

Choose an area of a living or dead tree where a branch has grown and cut the branch as close to the trunk as possible. Here you will find at least a few inches of fatwood. To process this wood for starting a fire, locate the dark, orange-colored fatwood area and scrape this into fine shavings with the back of your knife. This material will ignite with an open flame or a ferrocerium rod.

Inner Bark

The inner bark of a pine tree can be used as a food source. It also holds many antiseptic properties and can even be used as an impromptu bandage. When dried, the inner bark can also be used to make slats for woven baskets.

Willow

Willow is a water indicator tree, since it only grows well in wet areas along river and stream banks, drainage areas, and lakesides. Willow wood is soft, good for carving, and one of the best materials for a hearth and spindle when making a bow-drill fire set.

Willow Leaves and Branches

Willow leaves and the inner bark contain salicin, which is one of the chemical compounds used in aspirin. A decoction of the inner bark will make a fairly good headache remedy, and chewing the leaves will alleviate a toothache.

Willow Inner Bark

Willow's inner bark can be used to make baskets and pack boards. The bark is best harvested in the spring and early summer when the bark is loose and can easily be pried from the tree with a wedge. The outer bark can then be separated by peeling the inner bark from it. As with most of these types of components, the outer bark is most workable when kept wet.

Poplar Outer Bark

During the spring, easily remove the outer bark by prying it from the sapwood with a wedge or your axe blade. You can use this bark to make bark containers from baskets to arrow quivers. To do this, make two circular cuts through the bark around the tree; the distance between the cuts should be the desired length of the piece. Then, to open the bark, make a vertical cut by inserting a wedge between the bark and sap. You can then slowly peel off the outer bark.

Poplar Inner Bark

In the eastern woodlands, the inner bark of the poplar is one of the most prized resources next to pine sap. The inner bark provides both bird's nest material and tinder bundles for fire. When harvested green, it also makes a strong reverse wrap for two-ply cordages. Many times the inner bark fibers can easily be seen through rotting bark hanging off the branches. If branches are dead but not shedding, the back of your knife will easily process this to make the inner bark accessible.

POPLAR LEAF

"Nature's Priority: Take care of the brain first.
Then it will take care of you."

—GENE FEAR, *SURVIVING THE UNEXPECTED
WILDERNESS EMERGENCY*

Red Oak

Red oak is great for any building materials like slat boards and dimensional lumber. Red oak is a fibrous wood that handles bending stress easily, so it can also be used for making bows. Red oak can be used to heat-form many supplies, such as pack frames and snowshoe frames.

White Oak

White oak represents the medicinal side of the oak family. The inner bark of white oak can help relieve sinus congestion and headaches. Due to the high level of tannins, the leaves and the barks of this tree are very astringent and can be used medicinally for drawing infection or for driving things to the surface, like the oils from poison ivy, and for relieving diarrhea. White oak is antiseptic in nature, so decoctions of this bark make excellent mouthwashes and gargles for sore throat or gum problems.

Oak

Birch

There are several species of birch throughout the eastern woodlands, but black and river birch are the most prevalent in the middle ground areas of the Ohio River Valley. All birches contain oil that can be extracted from the bark, and it is so flammable that it can often still burn even when damp. Birch is an excellent carving wood and is the preferred material for Scandinavian-made knife handles.

Birch

Birch Bark

Birch bark provides probably the most versatile and even lifesaving resources of all the trees in the eastern woods, save maybe the pine. With its rich and volatile oils, birch bark burns with a dark black smoke that in the summer can help drive off insects. It is virtually unmatched in its ability to burn in damp conditions, and when using open flame it requires almost no processing to quickly create a hot, warming fire while drying marginal tinder as it goes.

Crafting Birch Bark

Birch bark is prized as a material for crafting containers of all sorts and for weaving to make baskets and sheaths. It is best to harvest the bark from live trees between May and June, but this tree is so resilient and resistant to rot that bark can even be harvested from dead trees. It is possible to harvest the outer bark without killing a live tree as long as you are able to do so without disturbing the inner bark. Make test cuts to determine the thickness and pliability of the bark before making large harvests.

Tinder Fungus

Birches that grow at higher altitudes or in colder climates are suscep-tible to a parasitic fungus commonly called tinder fungus (Inonotus obliquus), or chaga. Chaga grows in areas of the United States from New England and Michigan down to North Carolina. Chaga has long been sought for both its medicinal and fire tinder properties. It appears as a large blackened ball or mass on the side of the trunk of both live and fallen birch.

Birch Oil

Birch oil is extracted by using two containers of metal or clay. The first, called the catchment container, is buried below ground to the rim and surrounded by dirt. The second container is filled with birch bark and sealed with a drain hole or holes in the bottom from which oil drains into the catchment container. This container is placed just over the catchment container. A fire is then built around the aboveground container to heat the material and release the oils until they slowly drain into the container below.

Chaga

This fungus has extensive medicinal value; many woodsmen will simply boil a chunk of it in their kettle as a daily tea to drink at camp. When it's used as a fire starter, the yellow soft areas beneath the black outer crust will take the sparks from both steel and rod and will hold an ember to be used for ignition. You can slice it thinly or create a dust that can then be stored in your kit for later use.

Stone Boiling

Stone boiling is a process for disinfecting water or cooking food without a metal or nonflammable container. To stone boil you will need to heat rocks in a fire until they are glowing hot and then transfer them to the container of water in order to bring it to boiling temperature. Avoid using rocks found near water or porous rocks such as limestone. Look for rocks that are about fist size or a bit smaller.

Infusion

This process is just like making tea. The portions of the plant to be used are placed in water that has already been boiled and removed from the fire. A lid is placed on the container and the mixture is left to steep for 15–30 minutes. It is then consumed as needed.

Decoction

With a decoction, while boiling water you add bark or roots while the water is still on the fire and simmer until half the liquid remains. Then add to the original amount again and repeat. Once you have essentially twice-boiled the liquid, it can be strained and consumed or used as needed. Note: This method is always used for extraction from bark and roots.

Fomentation

A fomentation is an infusion or decoction in which a cotton material has been steeped for about 5 minutes and is then wrapped or placed on the skin.

Wash

You use a wash of either an infusion or decoction to wash or irrigate an area. You can also possibly soak something in it, such as your feet.

Poultice

A poultice is usually the macerated plant wrapped against the skin with a bandage. This method is used mainly for drawing infection or to reduce swelling.

Look at the Leaves

If you are having problems identifying a tree in the winter months when you have only the bark to examine, look on the ground around the tree. The leaves around it, even if dry, will be a good indicator of what type of tree it is.

Water Vines

Keep an eye out for water vines. In an emergency, if water is unavailable, wild grape or water vines will hold water for several months from early spring through summer. Cut the vine close to the ground first and then about 2' higher. A large vine will hold up to a cup of water.

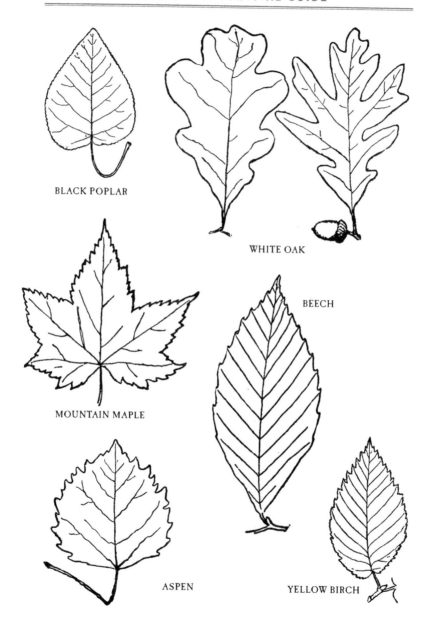

BLACK POPLAR

WHITE OAK

BEECH

MOUNTAIN MAPLE

ASPEN

YELLOW BIRCH

Dry Wood

Wood will dry out and crack faster once the bark is removed. This can be both an advantage and disadvantage, depending on the project for which you are collecting wood. You may want the wood to form a crack, which will make it easier to split.

Anvil Stump

Find a large stump if you can, or just cut off a piece of log that is large enough for a seat. This stump will keep you off the ground and will also function as a workbench and a dry surface on which to process fire tinder and kindling. The anvil stump can also be used much like a sawhorse when you add V notches on the side into which you can place pieces of wood that need to be cut. The anvil stump provides a raised surface for a candle at night as well.

Spear or Gig

Construct a spear of a hardwood sapling such as maple at least 12" taller than eye level when finished. Make a stout fork that has tines about 4" long on one end. If you are close to a good water source, such as a flowing stream or pond, make a gig on the other end by splitting the end of the sapling in a cross fashion to create four equal tines, each of which are about 6"–8" long. Then sharpen the stick as if it were still one solid piece. After this, two small green sticks will be placed into the crosscuts to force open the tines.

Maul or Mallet

A maul can be fashioned from a cut green hardwood branch. Mauls vary in size; start with a branch that is approximately 16" long and 4" in diameter. Carve the head from the first 6" of the branch and reduce the other end of the cut wood so that it comfortably fits in the hand, making its weight forward like a large, round hammer. Use this tool especially for striking the back of a metal tool such as your knife or axe. This tool will transform your axe into a wedge or a chisel.

Wedges

Wedges should be made from green hardwood material and, as with most of these tools, should be made in varying diameters and angles. Wedges can be used for splitting longer logs to make things like bow staves or dimensional lumber. They're also useful for separating bark from sapwood to make containers or bark shingles for roofing materials. When not in use, wedges can double as tent stakes. Fashion six separate wedges about 1"–2" in diameter and at least 12" long. In this way, these tools become one of the five simple machines you use most often in the woods.

Windlass

The windlass, used to move heavy weights or for tensioning, consists of a horizontal cylinder rotated by the turn of a crank or belt. A winch is affixed to one or both ends and a cable or rope is wound around the winch, pulling a weight attached to the opposite end. Make one more simply with a loop of cord or rope anchored to a fixed object and then looped around another object to be moved. Place a lever of proportionate size within the loop and turn, end over end, to tighten the line until it eventually moves the object.

Inclined Plane

An inclined plane is a simple machine for moving heavy objects above ground. The inclined plane takes advantage of angles in order to lever or pull weight forward on a shallow angle. This makes it easier to lift than pulling dead weight directly from the ground. You can, for example, move a larger log onto a sawhorse or pull a log uphill. To operate the inclined plane you take advantage of the hill and the log as a cylindrical rolling object. From there, you use a windlass to control the task of raising the log uphill.

Pulling a Log Uphill

To pull a log uphill, you will take advantage of the inclined plane of the hillside. You will need a length of rope long enough to form a W with the center wrapped around a tree at the top of the hill and the two outside Vs wrapping the log. The tails on the outside are used at the top to roll the log up the hill, with two people pulling at the same time.

Lever and Fulcrum

A lever made of strong material like green hardwood can be used not only to roll large logs and stones across the ground but also to assist in rolling logs up an inclined plane. When using a fulcrum in conjunction with a lever, you can also lift logs and other heavy objects.

Oil Wooden Tools

Any wooden tool will need to be oiled to keep it from drying out over time. Use animal fats or birch oil for this task. When a wooden tool is first made, you should oil it at least every day for a week, every week for a month, and every month for a year.

Primitive Fire-Starting

You should have three items for ignition in supply at all times:

- Lighter
- Ferrocerium rod
- Magnification lens (sunglass)

Cattails As Food

The center of the cattail shoot is a nutrient-dense, edible resource that makes an excellent vegetable you can simmer in soups or sauté as a side dish. Harvest the cattail shoots in dry weather so that the ground is not too muddy. Select large stalks that have not begun to flower, and separate the outer leaves from the core of the stalk. Discard these tough outer layers until you get down to the soft center. The product is delicious and rich in vitamins, including vitamin C, beta-carotene, and potassium.

Five Methods of Fire-Starting

There are five fire-starting methods in which every woodsman should be competent: open flame (lighter), ferrocerium rod, magnification lens, flint and steel, and bow and drill. These will ensure that the woodsman is prepared and can be comfortable, or "smooth it," in a woodland environment.

The Triangle of Fire

To create fire you need three key elements known as the triangle of fire: heat, oxygen, and fuel. To create the smoldering coal, your bow and drill set must take maximum advantage of all three. Methods in survival are like processes of manufacturing in that all inputs will affect the output. It is crucial that you ensure many things happen— and in the correct order—so that you get the desired output.

Bow and Drill Set

The bow and drill set has four components:

- Spindle or drill
- Hearth board
- Bearing block
- Bow

Used correctly, these components work as a simple machine that removes material and causes a fine dust to accumulate. The dust is then heated by the drill's friction, at which point oxygen in the surrounding air will allow ignition.

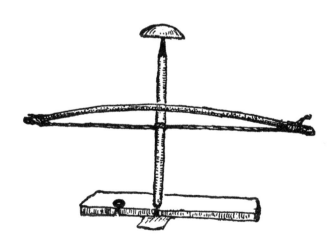

Making the Spindle

Make the spindle for your bow and drill set from a softwood. The spindle needs to be about the same diameter as your thumb and the length from your outstretched thumb to pinky. It should be as straight and round as possible. One end of the drill should look like a worn eraser on a pencil: slightly rounded. The top of the spindle is a pointed shape, but slightly dull. Make sure there is very little friction at the top of the spindle so that you can push and pull the bow easily.

Hearth Board

The hearth board for your bow and drill should be made from the same softwood as the spindle. The wood should be dry but not in a state of decay. You will want your finished hearth board to be about as long as your forearm and as thick as your thumb. Select a limb or piece of wood larger than what you need so that you can split it down to make a flat board with these dimensions.

Bearing Block

The bearing block for the bow and drill should be made from the hardest wood available, such as hickory or beech. Select a green sapling that is about 3" in diameter and cut out a 4"–5" piece on the widest end. Then split one-third off the sapling using your knife. Use your knife to create a small divot on the flat side of this block, right in the middle. The divot only needs to be large enough to accept the point of the spindle.

Bow

The bow for a bow and drill set can be made from any branch and does not have to necessarily be bent like a bow, but it needs to be fairly stiff so that it does not break under strain. The bow should be about 3' long and ½" in diameter. Making the bow is as simple as tying a string to a branch. The string does not need to be so tight that it causes the bow to bend in order to load the spindle, but the string cannot be so loose that the drill slips under downward pressure.

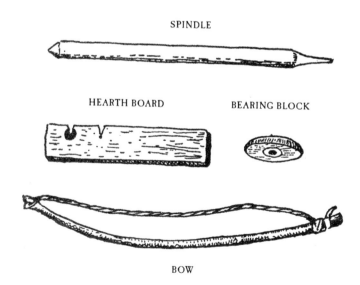

SPINDLE

HEARTH BOARD

BEARING BLOCK

BOW

The Bird's Nest

The ember that you ignite with your bow and drill will be used to ignite a bird's nest, a key part of your fire lay. The inner barks of the poplar or willow, or bark from the cedar, all work well, as do small dead pine needles and materials with a natural accelerant or highly combustible oils like birch bark. Don't use too much dry grass and leaves because these items burn quickly and it is important that the bird's nest burns long enough to ignite the rest of the fire lay materials.

Processing Material for the Bird's Nest—Step One

Processing means shredding barks to amass a quantity of fine material. Make sure you place something to catch the shreds so that they do not fall onto the ground. If the material you are collecting is still attached to the tree, use the back of your knife to process the shavings.

Processing Material for the Bird's Nest—Step Two

If the material is wet, process it immediately and spread it out over a larger surface to dry. You can place some of it between layers in the cloths around the core body area to dry them or spread them out on a dark surface in the sun.

"*The simpler the outfit, the more skill it takes to manage it, and the more pleasure one gets in his achievements.*"

—HORACE KEPHART, *CAMP COOKERY*

Using Your Bow and Drill—Step One

Place the spindle on the divot on the hearth board. Lock your wrist into your shin to prevent the spindle from moving side to side. Lean forward to put steady downward pressure on the spindle with the bearing block. Apply enough downward pressure to hold the drill in the divot as you slowly rotate the spindle. If you use the entire bow with steady strokes, downward pressure will create enough friction to begin burning the wood. Stop once the wood has burned around the spindle and things are running smoothly.

Using Your Bow and Drill—Step Two

Make a notch from the center of the freshly burned divot hole to the edge of the hearth board. The notch to the front of the board must face away from you because this will allow you to easily view the process when operating the drill. Take care the notch area is not too narrow. A proper notch should be in a V cut in which the bottom of the V goes approximately 1/8 the size of your burned divot circle into the blackened area. The angles of the V should be between 30°–45°.

Using Your Bow and Drill—Step Three

1. Check the bowstring for stretch and retighten if necessary.

2. Check the bearing block to make sure the divot is not getting too deep and that the spindle has not begun to shoulder out.

You need to make a welcome mat, a place for your coal to flow onto once it is created in the notch. The welcome mat can be a small sliver of bark or a thin piece of wood that is about two times as wide as the notch. This piece will go under the hearth board to catch the coal.

Using Your Bow and Drill—Step Four

Operate the bow slowly at first to establish and maintain a rhythm. Your chest should be over your knee so that you can easily observe the activity in the notch. Make steady, long strokes that use the entire length of the bow while you exert downward pressure. After several strokes you will begin to see smoke and the notch will start to fill with material. Once the material in the notch begins to spill forward in front of the notch you can increase the cadence of your bow strokes by about two to three times.

Using Your Bow and Drill—Step Five

Slow down during the last couple of strokes and stop in the position you started. Slowly remove the spindle and bow and observe the coal. If it seems to be smoking outside the board where the dust has gathered, you are probably home free. Don't get too excited though, because you still have about 5 or more minutes. Slowly lift the board at an angle and tap it gently with the spindle to dislodge any material that might be clogged in the notch. If the coal is still smoking at this point, you can sit back and relax for a minute.

Using Your Bow and Drill—Step Six

Always bring the bird's nest to the coal—never the other way around. Make any necessary adjustments to your bird's nest to make sure there is plenty of fine combustible material in the middle. Tilt the nest toward the welcome mat and pick up the welcome mat, moving it toward the nest. Then slowly tap the welcome mat to dump the coal into the nest. This should only be a ¼" drop at most! Slightly fold the nest and begin to add some oxygen by breathing into it slightly, not hard blows just light breaths.

Using Your Bow and Drill—Step Seven

If the coal is still burning strongly, you can tilt the nest slightly so that you are blowing up into it, causing the heat to rise into the bulk of the nest. As the ember grows, smoke will begin to roll from the back of the nest, which is the cue for you to blow a bit harder. As the smoke thickens you can increase the oxygen until it begins to burn. Once the nest starts to flame, turn it over so the flames are on the bottom and heat rises to the nonburning material. Finally, place it into your fire lay and make a fire!

Material for Flint and Steel Ignition

Some fungi such as chaga will take the spark from flint and steel without your having to char it first. You can also get dust from some types of shelf fungus to accept a spark. To accomplish this, you will require a small pile of dust that you have created with a saw cut or by scraping with the back of the knife. Once the dust has ignited, leave it to grow into a coal. Chaga can be ignited within a larger piece and the dust is not necessary. With either, use the softer, inner materials, not the outer, hard surface.

Making Char–Step One

The easiest way to make char is to place your chosen material in a metal chamber where you can subject it to high heat while limiting oxygen. In this chamber, gases are able to escape as the material is heated inside. A stainless-steel bottle and nesting cup will work nicely, or in an emergency even an old can with a flat rock. Place your material inside the chamber and then place the chamber in the fire. Coals are better than direct flame but either will work.

Making Char—Step Two

As the material is heated in the metal chamber, gas will begin to escape the chamber from any place that is not completely sealed. This is okay so long as oxygen cannot enter the chamber. Once the smoke stops, the charring is complete. Wait until the chamber is completely cool before opening it because if oxygen contacts hot material it will cause it to burn. Inspect the char. If it is black and frail looking, it is most likely ready. If the material is brown, close the chamber and put it back into the fire.

Char Tins

Many woodsmen carry a specific container such as an Altoids tin or an old shoe polish can, called a char tin, for fire material and charring. Strike sparks from the metal tool directly into the tin, which increases the surface area for catching an ember. Once an ember is created, place it into the bird's nest as described for the bow-drill fire.

Solar Fire

A sunglass can ignite any char material or various fungus species. Horse hoof fungus may work better as a dust, but it will make a nice coal in a short amount of time. You can also create an ember by compressing natural materials such as cattail down or poplar barks into a small, tight ball about ¼" in diameter. Then use the glass to burn into the material, creating a smoldering ember.

Matches

Matches are extremely sensitive to weather and moisture, and you can only carry so many. It would take several boxes of matches to come close to the open-flame power and longevity of a single BIC cigarette lighter. The one small advantage of matches may be the tiny amount of tinder a wooden match requires, but this is negligible in a proper fire lay.

Collect Rocks

Always keep an eye out for rocks that may be hard enough to drive a spark from high-carbon tools. Pick up rocks as you are walking and try them. If they work, throw them in your pack; if not, toss them aside. Chert and flint will have a slick shine to them when wet and may be white, gray, or pale hues of red and pink; quartz will always be a good bet.

Candle Stub

A small stub from a used candle is always a good safety device to have when fire starting. Light the candle with the first open flame and set it aside until the fire has become sustainable. If you need a longer open flame for marginal materials, this will save precious lighter fluid. Candles are much easier to make than a new lighter.

Assembling Your Kit

Even if you intend to build a base camp with a permanent shelter, you might still need to travel for a night or two to hunt, trap, or fish. For this reason, your kit should include a system that takes you easily from cabin to woods with supplies that will be useful in either situation. The base of this kit will include:

- Waterproof tarp (Egyptian cotton oilcloth works well here)

- Wool blanket

- Simple sleeve of canvas (like a painter's canvas) if you plan to make a raised bed

The Four Ws of Shelter

There are four critical elements to consider when looking for a place to build your shelter:

- Wind

- Water

- Wood

- Widowmakers

Wind

The direction of the wind will have an impact on your ability to safely keep a fire going and heat your shelter. Look for middle high-ground areas where the wind is present but not too strong.

Water

Look for a nearby area such as a creek bed that can supply a steady source of water.

Wood

You will need a lot of wood for the fire, building shelter, and making other resources. A large fallen tree provides a good source of firewood, and trees such as pines can provide a steady supply of fatwood.

Widowmakers

Examine the trees around you—especially large trees—very carefully for any dead branches that could pose a danger to you and your campsite.

Permanent Shelter

For your permanent shelter, you can either build a larger version of
your temporary base camp (like a hunter's station) from natural
materials, or you can pack a larger canvas shelter in your kit. Which-
ever you choose, it must have at least three sides for protection from
inclement weather and a large fire backing or portable wood stove
that is at least as high as the pitch or roof of the shelter. In colder
weather a raised bed is a must, but if the weather is fair, a hammock
may be enough.

Small Wall Tents

Small wall tents can be very comfortable and offer great protection
from the elements especially if a stove jack is installed. Within the
wall tent you can easily fit a hammock, a cot, or even build a raised
bed. The wall tent provides coverage on all four sides, which makes
it operate like a canvas cabin. An 8' × 10' wall tent provides plenty
of room for one person. It can be used temporarily with all the same
fixtures and amenities, such as lighting and sleep setups, which you
will eventually use for a more permanent shelter.

Open-Faced Tents

Remember that large canvases can be difficult to heat, so for a seasonal shelter, think about selecting something small. Much of the decision about what type of canvas shelter to use will depend on your environment. Open-faced tents like the Whelen provide three sides of coverage and can be used with a hammock. For colder weather I would recommend something that can house a stove, like a small wall tent.

Securing Your Shelter

There are many methods for securing your shelter, all of which depend on the materials that were used to manufacture it and the environmental conditions in which it has been erected. Stay away from grommets; they seem to be the weakest link in any shelter because they tend to weaken the surrounding fabric. Instead, opt for the tie-out or stake loops. If you have only a blank canvas with no way to tie it off, place a toggle on the corners and fold it over the toggle; trap this with a jam knot on the corner of the tarp.

Tie Lines

All tie lines should be made adjustable for tension so they can be tightened or loosened when necessary. To do this, use flat slabs of wood with a hole drilled on each end that is large enough for the ropes to pass through. Place the rope in this toggle, one end in each hole, and knotted. If you are using loops for tie-out points, pass the rope through the loop before knotting on one end of this sliding toggle. After this it can be looped over a stake and then adjusted for tension.

Metal Stakes

If the ground is extremely hard, fashion stakes from a 3/8" steel stock like rebar with a 2" × 120° bend at the top. If stakes are not practical at all, you can improvise with things like logs, rocks, or bags filled with something heavy like smaller rocks or dirt. If the ground is extremely soft, it may take a chain of two stakes to secure the tent in high wind conditions.

"Shelter provides a microenvironment that supplements inadequate clothing or allows you to shed cumbersome layers, especially when you want to stop moving or when you want to sleep in cold weather. Shelter also enhances the effect of a warming fire."

—MORS KOCHANSKI

Caves and Rock Houses

Long before man started constructing his own shelter, he adopted existing elements in nature to be his home, just as animals do. These caves and stone shelters endure in nature, and although it takes a little effort to make them comfortable, they can still be a great choice if the situation arises. In fact, there are millions of people worldwide who live in cave dwellings.

The Downside of Caves

It is important to remember the dangers that may present themselves in natural dwellings. A wet cave can be a miserable place to sleep. If you are in an area with high humidity or lots of annual rainfall, caves are not the best choice. Cave moisture creates several dangers, including bacteria growth, mold, weak stone integrity of the cave itself, and a dampness that could leave you cold most of the time. A cave might also already be home to insects and other mammals such as bats, cats, or bears.

Raised Platform Shelters

A raised platform shelter can be constructed by attaching wood pieces with simple lashings and cross members to create the platform. The raised platform should be at least 3'–5' above ground level; again, this depends on the factors like wildlife, resources, and environment. Make this platform at least 2' wider than the inside dimension of the shelter you plan to place on top of it and at least 6' longer to leave room for open work areas. The covering or construction of the shelter itself can be a simple hoop design or a square structure.

Log Cabins

Building a small cabin with a single pitched roof is a fairly simple undertaking from a design perspective. However, it is labor-intensive and requires a great deal of timber resources. An 8' × 10' cabin should be sufficient for a single person. Anything larger will be difficult to heat. You will want logs of at least 8"–10" diameter for this, and size will dictate the number needed.

Earthen Structures

Shelters constructed from earthen materials are a good option if the resources are available. Partial wood construction shelters can also be covered with earthen materials for far better insulation in cold-weather environments.

Sod

Sod makes good shelter coverage because it should continue growing foliage over time, which will only add to its waterproofing and insulation capabilities. Sod can be cut to any width and length but should always be at least 4" thick. If you intend to use sod materials on a roof, ensure that the supporting structure can hold the weight before covering. You will want semi-clear sod that does not contain small trees or bushes, which may later grow large roots that interfere with the rest of the structure.

Materials for Natural Cements

The following materials are required to make natural cement:

- Clay-based soil (if the soil feels smooth and slick when wet, it most likely has a higher clay content)

- Grasses and longer fibers that can be used as rebar

- A source of water

- A bucket or container for mixing

Making Cement—Step One

To make the cement, collect enough clay-based soil to fill your bucket. You will also need a good armload of dry grasses about 6"–12" long or other fibrous plant materials. Long, dry grasses work much better than green grass for this project. Now mix some water with the clay until you get a squishy consistency that is not too runny. If you are using this for a mortar or chink, mix it thinner. You can mix the cement right in the bucket, but a tarp works very well for this process.

Making Cement—Step Two

Spread out the tarp, lay down the grasses, and dump the mud on top
of them. The most effective way to incorporate the mix is with your
bare feet so that the materials grind together. You can fold the tarp
over the materials and walk on the enclosed mass, or you can simply
use your hands to make sure the grasses are well mixed and nothing
is left dry or unmixed. Use the cement immediately to create your
structure or as mortar for your project. If you want to save it for
later, you can shape it into bricks.

Lantern

A simple lantern can be fashioned from an empty can to protect the candle from going out in the wind. If your hunting or trapping campaign has been successful, use fat from the animal to make oil lamps. Any concave container, from a shell to a hollow piece of wood, will make an easy lamp. All you need is a wick, which can be made from any soluble material such as cotton rope or natural cordage. You can also use a ball of compressed cattail fluff or corded cedar bark for a quick, temporary wick.

Candles

Make candles by dipping a wick of natural cord into a pan of melted tallow, letting it cool, dipping again, and letting it cool. The thickness increases each time. The difference between tallow and lard is the tallow will harden at room temperature and lard will stay soft. Torches are easily made by dipping the tops of dead plants such as mullein into fat and letting them dry.

Soap

Many plants have natural saponins, chemicals that are created by the saponification process when making soaps. This substance occurs naturally in many plants and creates a nice lather that can be used as a natural soap. In the eastern woodlands, the best choice for this is the bracken fern because its root is high in saponins. Yucca is another American plant that can be used for this purpose.

BRACKEN FERN

Latrine

The pit latrine should be as deep as possible but should be kept to at least 3' above the water table. If you find yourself needing to choose between a farther walk and possible groundwater pollution, do yourself a favor and take the walk uphill. A good practice for wilderness pit latrines is to add ashes from the campfire daily. This will cover the smell, break down the fecal matter, and detract pests such as flies. Once the pit is full within a foot of the top, cover it with debris and dig a new pit in a different location.

Lines

Ridgelines are the best place to hang a lantern, keep clothing off the ground, or suspend a bag of goodies that may be needed at night. Drying lines should always be used to ensure you have a place to air bedding material and clothing during the day or when wet. Beating a wool blanket hung over a line will keep it free of dirt, dead skin cells, and many pests.

Sleep System

Sleeping gear can have a big impact on the weight of your supplies—
a simple canvas and a couple of wool blankets can add as much as
20 pounds to your kit. Still, a good night's sleep of at least 6 hours is
one of the most important aspects of long-term comfort and survival.
Often my sleep system makes up two-thirds of my kit's weight.

Sleeping Gear

Be sure to have:

- Wool blanket (or two)
- Materials for a raised bed
- Canvas
- Large needle, like a sail needle, that is heavy enough
  to puncture your canvas
- #36 bank line for stitching the canvas
- Synthetic sleeping bag

Building a Raised Bed

First fold a heavy canvas widthwise (not lengthwise). Thread your needle with the #36 bank line and whipstitch the ends of your canvas together on two sides. The stitching does not have to be perfect; anything between 1"–2" stitches will work fine. Next, stuff your bed with leaves and grass. Stuff the bed and then compress the material to make room for more. Stuff the bed again and compress the material to make room for more. When the bed is packed with about 4" of compressed insulation, stitch up the last side with your whipstitch.

Underquilts

Hammocks require an underquilt or some sort of insulation to battle convection issues in colder weather. Place a thick pad like a ground mat in the hammock and a reflective batting on top of that. Then place your sleeping bag or blankets right on this pad. Reflectix is an insulation used for the home and can be purchased at any hardware store. It comes in 2'–3' widths and is basically Bubble Wrap with Mylar covering. The other option is an underquilt that will trap warm air between the quilt and the hammock.

*"Bushcraft is what you carry in your mind
and your muscles."*

—RAY MEARS

Treating Canvas

Canvas that is untreated may be susceptible to mold. Treating it before use with a guarding agent is prudent. Canvas can also be very susceptible to UV breakdown at altitudes of about 3,000', so treat it or buy Sunforger tent canvas, which will be the best bet for a long-lasting shelter.

Setting Up Your Sleep Area

Fold over your tarp and lay it down where it will act as a moisture barrier between the ground and your raised bed. The wool blanket will keep you warm while sleeping. Carry some sort of bag—even your haversack—that can be emptied at night and filled with spare clothing to act as a pillow. A pillow is a tremendous comfort that is often completely underrated.

Insulation

Remember that any insulation made from natural material on the ground to battle conduction should be 4" thick when compressed.

Cordage and Ropes

For long-term excursions, here are the most beneficial and multi-functional ropes and materials:

- Natural ropes
- Paracord
- Bank line
- Natural strings
- Webbing
- Mule tape

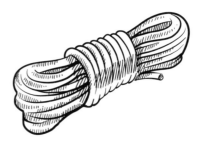

Natural Rope versus Synthetic Rope

Natural rope is easier to use and far more versatile than most synthetics. This is true especially when it is broken down into smaller fibers or cords. Synthetic ropes, such as rigging rope or Kevlar climbing and static-line ropes, are widely available and can be a good resource to keep on hand if you have room in your kit. Just know that while these synthetics are strong for their relative size, the fibers tend to break down after lengthy exposure in the wilderness, which makes them difficult to use.

Conserving Cordage

Whether it is synthetic rope you have carried in your kit or natural rope you have manufactured yourself, cordage is a precious resource that should be treated with care. When working with synthetic rope, avoid cutting lengths shorter than about 20', or four "pulls" from the roll, unless it is absolutely necessary. One "pull" is the length of your outstretched arms, from one hand to the other. For this reason, it is always best to use natural bark cordage for small binding or lashing projects.

Making Rope

You can make a rope by combining and twisting three or more strands together. There are three components to a rope:

- Fibers: The fibers are the smallest materials that are twisted together to create the yarns.

- Yarns: Yarns are multiple fibers twisted together in the same direction.

- Strands: Strands are multiple yarns again twisted in a single direction.

Rope Twisting—Step One

Rope is made from multiple strands twisted in two different directions. It only takes one person to operate a simple rope twister, which can produce lengths of rope that are about 20' long. To make enough, you will need to feed about eleven times the amount of cord you intend to produce through the rope twister. Attach one end of the cord to a stationary object and make one loop so that you can attach it to the spinner and twist. Start by spinning in a clockwise fashion until the cord begins to wind on itself when it is slack.

Rope Twisting—Step Two

Divide the cord in thirds and make two loops: one to place over the original stationary object and one to place around the twister. You should now have three strands of larger cord again between the twister and the static end. Begin spinning again in counterclockwise fashion until the desired tightness is achieved. Once the rope is finished, pull hard against the static object to "set" the rope. Cut the ends and whipstitch them to finish your rope.

Stop Knots

The stop knot is used as a security knot in conjunction with jamming and joining knots. Both joining and jamming knots are used to join two cords or ropes together to increase cordage length. A stop knot is an overhand knot that is tied to keep the line from slipping under tension, passing back through a hole, or even slipping through another knot.

Jamming Knots

A jamming knot is used to join two pieces of cordage of the same diameter together, especially if the line to be extended has a loop on the end. The beauty of these knots is how easily they can be loosened for adjustment or removal on the fly or in a hurry.

Slip Loop or Hitch Loop

The slip loop is used to make a tension device, kind of like a pulley. It is used for things like holding loads tight or pulling a ridgeline taut. The slip loop can be easily incorporated into the standing line and comes undone with a simple pull.

Barrel Knots/Blood Knots

Barrel knots can be used on one side of a standing or looped line to create a slider that can be adjusted for tensioning guy lines. If it is tied on two opposing lines, it becomes a joining or blood knot. The blood knot is often used for monofilament or fishing lines.

End-of-Line Loops

These knots are simply used to create a loop tied in one end of a line or rope. This can be used as an attachment point or a tensioning loop around an object as when you are putting up a ridgeline around a tree.

Figure Eight

Figure-eight loops create end-of-line loops that are easily broken or untied after tension is applied to the loop. These loops work much better than a simple overhand knot to create end-of-line loops.

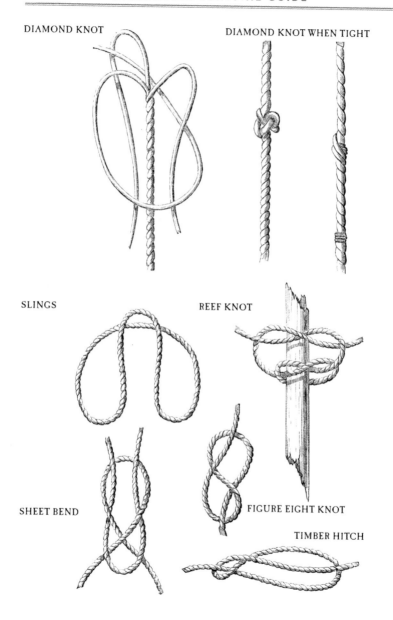

DIAMOND KNOT

DIAMOND KNOT WHEN TIGHT

SLINGS

REEF KNOT

SHEET BEND

FIGURE EIGHT KNOT

TIMBER HITCH

LOOP SLIP

CARRICK BEND

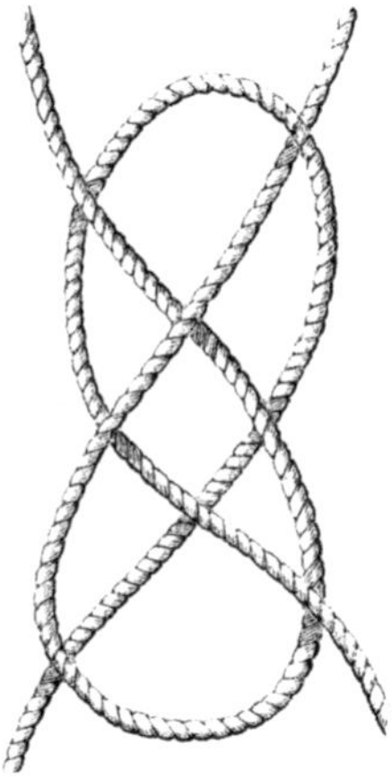

HALF HITCH

CLOVE HITCH

TIMBER HITCH

BOWLINE KNOT

Bowline

The bowline is an end-of-line loop that has a few advantages over the others. For one, it tightens or constricts against the line as tension is applied, which makes it a good rescue loop. It can also easily be tied into the line after the rope is already passing around another object.

Slippery Hitch

The slippery hitch is a quick hitch to secure objects that are not under a load. It could be used when hanging a cord from another line or a branch. It is a quick-release knot so it is especially helpful for things such as tying a line from a boat to a tree on the shore.

Timber Hitch

The timber hitch is a great starting hitch for any lashings because it is a constricting knot that relies on friction in order to hold. It can be easily undone to recover cordage and can be used at the end of bowstrings.

Trucker's Hitch

The trucker's hitch incorporates an in-line loop to secure a load or a tensioned line. It can be set up to quick-release so that loads can be easily untied or so that ridgelines at the campsite can be easily moved.

Bindings

Bindings are a combination of wraps, knots, and hitches that are used for securing something. They can be used to secure loads that will be transported over a distance or to secure a series of contents rolled into a package such as a tarp or blanket. They can even be used to attach a bundle to something else such as a pack frame, horse, or sled.

"Whoever coined the saying 'an ounce of prevention is worth a pound of cure' must have been thinking about survival."

—BRIAN EMDIN, *SURVIVAL SECRETS*

Basket Weaving

Make a cross lashing in a square-lash fashion with four flexible
twigs, shoots, or splits on each side for a total of eight sticks. You
will need to add a ninth stick as you begin to weave your basket.
You can weave in vines, bark, or splits. Weave in and out of the
splits. Shape this weave into a basket by gradually lifting the sides
and controlling the tightness of the weave to form a round container.
Finish by wrapping another piece of the material in an overhand
running-stitch fashion around the top and trim any excess sticks
or twigs.

Simple Coil Basketry

It takes a good amount of cordage to sew a coil basket—especially a
large one—but the materials used to make the coils are quite simple.
Choose items that can be doubled in half without breaking, such as
pine needles and other leaves. Then you will need some bank line and
a shuttle or a needle. Start with a section of the material you plan to
coil. Double it over and wrap it into a tube, and then make progressive
coils in a circular fashion, wrapping or sewing with the bank line to
hold them together.

Bark Baskets—Step One

Score the outer bark of a yellow poplar down to the sapwood with
a knife or axe. Then score another line in a circular fashion above
and below that first line and use a sharp stick or spud to peel it
away from the tree. Cut a piece of bark two and a half times longer
than the finished basket needs to be high. Cut two half-moons on
the outside of the bark right in the middle of your piece. The half-
moons should be facing each other so that their bottom and top tips
are touching.

Bark Baskets—Step Two

These cuts you just made are the fold lines that form the bottom of
the basket. You can then fold up the sides and lace them. Fold up the
piece with the bark facing out, and drill holes up the sides using your
awl. Use strong cordage to lace up the basket with simple x stitches.
Add a handle to the top if needed. Yellow poplar is my favorite for
this, but you can also use birch.

Weaving

Weaving is a broad skill that can produce anything from straps for a backpack to baskets or even shelter coverings. It can be as simple as weaving together small strands of cordage or as complex as using a loom to weave threads into a wide textile.

Weaving Terms

- CROSSHATCH—Two series of parallel lines that flow in opposite directions so that they cross each other.

- WARP—The set of lengthwise threads on a loom.

- WEFT—The thread that is drawn through the warp threads to create a textile.

- SHED—The separation between the upper and lower warp threads.

- HEDDLE—The part of the loom that separates the warp threads so that the weft can be threaded through them.

- SHUTTLE—Anything that will carry the weft across the warp and through the shed.

Diagonal Finger Weaving–Step One

Place two nails about 6" apart in a piece of stationary wood such as a workbench. Your weaving stick will rest on top of these nails while you work. Select a weaving stick about ½ in diameter and 12"–16" long. Double five strands of cord, such as jute string, over the weaving stick and secure each cord with a lark's head knot. You will then have ten strands hanging off your weaving stick.

Diagonal Finger Weaving–Step Two

Use a second stick, similar in diameter and length to your weaving stick, as a winding stick and place it below the two nails that are holding your weaving stick. Wrap finished product around the winding stick as you weave. Now set your weaving stick on top of the nails. Loop the tenth strand over the right-hand nail in your workbench. Take the first strand, your active strand, and loop it under the second stand, over the third strand, under the fourth strand, over the fifth . . . until you reach the ninth strand. Then take the tenth strand off the nail and replace it with your active strand.

Diagonal Finger Weaving–Step Three

For the second row, take what is now your first strand and loop it over the second strand, under the third strand, over the fourth strand . . . until you reach the ninth strand.

Pull the tenth strand off the nail and replace it with your active strand. Continue this process, taking the first strand in the line and alternating the under/over weave and then switching that pattern in the next row to the opposite, until your piece reaches the desired length. At this time, take your tenth strand and fashion it into a clove hitch to finish the strap.

Cross Weaving

Cross weaving is a process that can be used with any textured material like barks or cattail leaves. Cross weaving involves hatching and can be used to make materials as large or as small as you need. It can also be shaped into almost any configuration needed. Picture a tic-tac-toe board in which the lines of the board alternate over and under each other to form a weave.

Woodland Loom—Step One

Secure one long sapling about waist high on a tree in a T fashion with a simple lashing. Place several stakes in the ground away from, but directly in front of, this crossbar. These stakes are your looming poles and should be lined up perpendicular to the tree. The longer the project, the farther the stakes should be placed. The width of your project will be determined by the number of stakes in the row.

Then create another bar from a similar size sapling as the one you used for the T. You now have the components of your loom.

Woodland Loom—Step Two

Alternate the warps for the weave with strong cordage so the first warp is fixed to the sapling you secured to the tree. The next warp is secured to a stake. The next warp is secured to the sapling on the tree. The one after that is secured to the next stake in the line. Continue setting up the warps in this pattern until the final stake. Use the crossbar as your heddle. Once the warps are complete, you will be able to raise and lower the heddle to place wefts of material in the loom, alternating over and under them. Use another sapling as a beater stick to tighten the wefts as you go.

Tablet Weaving—Step One

In tablet weaving, cards, or flat pieces into which holes have been drilled, operate as the shed. To begin, you will need to create an even number of square cards that are about 3" on all sides. For this you can use wood, cardboard, plastic, or any other material that is fairly stiff. Drill four holes, one in each corner, in each of your cards. These cards will act as the heddle, and one thread will pass through each of the holes to create the warps. So if you have twelve cards, you will have forty-eight warps.

Tablet Weaving–Step Two

The loom can be any two points to which you can attach your threads. When you begin weaving, either hold the end of the loom that is nearest to the cards or attach it to your belt. Secure the far end by a slipknot to a stationary object such as a tree. Take the number of warps and cut half that many strings. If you want forty-eight warps, cut twenty-four strings. Fold each string in half and secure to the near end of your loom with a lark's head knot. Once all the strings are attached, you can now thread each through the holes in your cards.

Tablet Weaving–Step Three

Once the warps are established you will need a shuttle. A net needle will work, or any needle that has an eye big enough to hold your cordage. Pass the shuttle through the shed, the gap between the top holes in your cards and the bottom holes. Once you reach the end of the line, turn your cards a quarter turn clockwise. Now pass the weft through the shed once more. Once you reach the end of the line, turn your cards another quarter turn clockwise. Repeat these steps until you reach the desired length.

"Something will have gone out of us as a people
if we ever let the remaining wilderness be
destroyed . . . We simply need that wild country
available to us, even if we never do more than
drive to its edge and look in."

—WALLACE STEGNER

A Simple Peg Loom

Simple peg looms are useful because they can be adjusted to work with materials of all sizes to make products of all dimensions. For the sake of our instructions, assume we are using wool yarn to make a scarf. When weaving with a peg loom, the string threaded through each peg is the warp. The yarn wrapped around each peg is the weft.

Constructing a Peg Loom

To build a peg loom you will need the following materials:

- 1 piece of wood: 2" × 4" and about 1'–2' long
- 8 dowel rods about 1" × 6"–8"
- A drill

Drill a series of holes into your 2" × 4" into which each of your dowel rods will sit. Drill a hole at the base of each peg through which you will thread the warp strings. These holes should be high enough that when the pegs are placed in the holes on the 2" × 4" you can see them above the edge.

Setting Up the Peg Loom—Step One

Determine how long you want your final product to be and use double
the amount of cordage. Now thread one piece of yarn through each
peg. Pull the yarn through until both sides of the yarn hang evenly
from the peg hole. These hanging yarns will operate as the warp. Now
that your peg loom is set up, it is time to begin weaving. Pull the tail
from your ball of yarn (or whatever material you are using) and tie
it to your first peg. Use an overhand knot that is secure and will not
come undone.

Setting Up the Peg Loom—Step Two

Pass the yarn behind the second peg, in front of the third peg, behind
the fourth peg, in front of the fifth peg, behind the sixth peg. Bring
your yarn back to the first peg by passing it in front of the sixth peg,
behind the fifth peg, in front of the fourth peg, behind the third peg,
in front of the second peg, and in front of your first peg. Now send
that yarn back down the line of pegs. Each row of wraps you make
around the pegs locks in the previous row of wraps because they
wind in the opposite direction.

Setting Up the Peg Loom—Step Three

Continue passing the weft around the pegs until your stacks of wraps
are about three-quarters of the way up your pegs. As you weave, push
down the rows of wraps with a beater stick or your hands. This not

only tightens up the rows on your work, but also allows you to fit more rows on the pegs.

Setting Up the Peg Loom—Step Four

Tie a slipknot in the bottom of the hanging yarns to make sure that the weaving holds together as you unload the pegs. Pull the pegs out of their holes and slip each stack of wraps off the pegs and slide them onto your hanging yarns. Put the pegs back into the holes and wrap the yarn around them again, alternating directions, until they reach about halfway or three-quarters of the way up the pegs. Once more, slip them off the pegs and slide them onto your weft. Continue doing this until the piece reaches your desired length.

"The more survival skills an individual has that have been practiced physically and otherwise, the better odds they have for those skills coming to the forefront during a stressful emergency."

—CODY LUNDIN,
98.6 DEGREES: THE ART OF KEEPING YOUR ASS ALIVE

Inkle Loom

An inkle loom is a tape loom that can be used to make narrow pieces such as belts, trim for clothing, haversack straps, and sashes. Constructing the inkle loom is challenging, but once set up and threaded, weaving on the loom is very straightforward and simple.

Making an Inkle Loom– Materials

To make an inkle loom you will need the following materials:

- 1 piece of wood 30" × 1" × 4"
- 3 pieces of wood 15" × 1" × 4"
- 1 piece of scrap wood 15"–20" long
- 1 piece of dowel rod about 32" long
- Wood glue
- 4 (1") wood screws; 8 (2") wood screws
- Drill with a #2 Phillips bit
- Saw

Making an Inkle Loom—Step One

Lay the 30" piece of wood on your workspace. Spread some wood glue on the flat end of your first 15" piece and place it at 15°–20° angle on the right flat end of the 30" board. Secure the wood by drilling in a couple of wood screws. Take the second 15" board and place it a foot away from the first on the 30" piece, at the same slight angle in the opposite direction. Secure with wood glue and a couple of screws. Attach the scrap wood at the bottom edge of your 30" piece, perpendicular to the 15" pieces.

Making an Inkle Loom—Step Two

Next, saw your dowel rod into pegs that are equal lengths of 6". You will need eight pegs for the inkle loom. Drill a ½"-deep hole in the bottom of each peg (I use a vise to hold the peg steady while drilling) and attach three of them to the flat side of each angled 15" piece of wood. The first peg on each piece of 15" wood should be attached 2" from the top, the second 2" from the bottom, and the third right in the middle—about 8" from the bottom.

Making an Inkle Loom—Step Three

To attach the pegs, put a little wood glue on the back of each peg and also on the screw threads. Attach the seventh peg to the front end of the 30" piece of wood just under the lowest peg on the first angled 15" board. Attach the last peg to the front of the third piece of 15" wood. Use a C-clamp to secure this piece of wood to the 30" board on the loom while you thread the pegs. This piece of wood will move back and forth as you begin operating the loom.

Threading the Inkle Loom—Step One

You will need two sets of cordage to weave on your inkle loom. I generally use a jute string and often two different colors, one for the warps and another for the weft, which produces an attractive pattern. Tie the tail of your first set of cordage to the 15" board that holds peg 8. Now bring your string over the top of pegs 1 and 2, under peg 3, over peg 4, under peg 5, over peg 6, skip the heddle peg (7), and under peg 8.

Threading the Inkle Loom—Step Two

Bring your string back to the top of the loom, but this time go under peg 1 and then again over 2, under 3, over 4, under 5, over 6, skip 7, and under 8. Bring the string to the top of the loom once more but this time string it over 1, over 2 . . . and so forth. Essentially you will be alternating your over/under for only peg 1. The direction of string for the other pegs will always remain the same.

Threading the Inkle Loom—Step Three

Continue to place the warps this way until you reach your desired project width. This space between the strings that were passed over peg 1 and those that were passed under peg 1 will create your shed, and your shuttle will pass through this space.

Weaving with an Inkle Loom

To begin weaving, attach your second supply of string to the warp strings in front of peg 8. Load your shuttle with the string. Attach with a simple clove hitch so you can easily undo the knot later. For the first row, push the warp strings in front of peg 1 down to make the shed. Pass your shuttle through this space. For the second row, push the warp strings in front of peg 1 up, and pass your shuttle through this space. Use your beater stick to push down each weft on the warps as you loom.

Rotating the Inkle Loom Piece

When the weft is about an inch away from the heddle, it is time to rotate your piece. Undo the clove hitch that you used to attach the weft to the loom and tie it around the warp strings, securing it with a tight overhand knot. Now that your second cordage is free from the loom, pull the work away from you and push the heddle strings up. Keep pulling the work backward and pushing the heddle strings up until the woven piece is winding under the loom and the warp in front of you is clear and ready to receive the weft.

Waist Looms

With a waist loom you can weave projects of unlimited length. The weaver uses himself as the base of the loom with a stick and a waist strap or two metal rings. The warps are separated by a warp loop, and then the heddle strings are attached to a floating stick. The warps can then be manipulated by lifting the warp or heddle string to open a shed. The weft is woven into the shed with a shuttle of your choosing. Use another stick to roll up the completed product as the weaving progresses.

Nets and Net Making

If you plan to spend time in an area with waterways, net making will prove to be one of the most valuable skills you will ever learn. You can make nets of any shape, size, or dimension to fit your needs. A good gill net (or stop net, as they are sometimes called) is a reliable source of food. Nets are wonderful to have on hand because they can also be multipurposed to cover and haul cargo or incorporated in land traps when capturing live food.

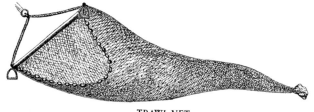

TRAWL NET

KEER DRAG NET

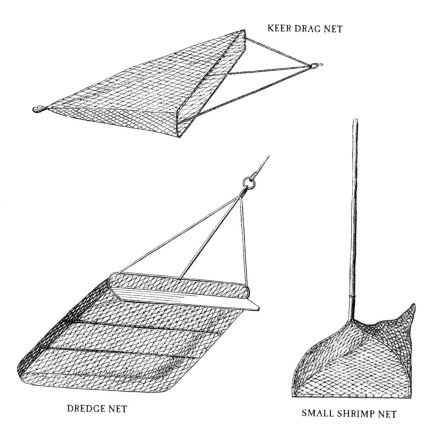

DREDGE NET

SMALL SHRIMP NET

Gill Nets

For net building you will need the following:

- Large quantity of cordage with a thin diameter (I prefer #6 bank line)

- Small amount of a thick cordage (like #36 bank line)

- Net needle (these can be handmade with pine or cedar but commercial versions are also available in plastic)

- Mesh gauge that is the same width as your net needle

Loading the Net Needle

First tie a clove hitch into your thin cordage and slip it over the point in your net needle. Flip the net needle to the back, bring the cordage down to the end of the net needle, wrap it around the base, bring it back up and wrap it around the point again, flip the net needle to the front, wrap the cordage around the base, back up around the center point, flip the needle to the back, and so forth until your cordage is loaded about three-quarters of the way up the point in your net needle.

Setting Up the Mesh—Step One

Tie your thick cordage to two stationary objects so that it stretches out at a height that is comfortable for you to begin working. This thicker cordage will act as your headline, and you will build your mesh by attaching the cordage from the net needle directly to this line. Pull line from the point of the net needle and attach it to the headline with a clove hitch.

Setting Up the Mesh—Step Two

You are now ready to secure your thin cordage to your headline with a series of knots. Using a mesh gauge ensures that every space in your mesh is the same width. Remember, the size of the spaces in your mesh determine what you will catch. If your spaces are 2" wide, anything that is smaller than 2" will be able to escape.

Setting Up the Mesh—Step Three

Bring your net needle line up at an angle and wrap it behind and over the headline and mesh gauge. Now bring the net needle line up again, but this time wrap it behind and over only the headline and make a knot around the loop you just made. Move like this, over the mesh gauge and headline, and then over just the headline and around your loop, until you have fifteen knots in your headline.

Setting Up the Mesh—Step Four

Now that the cord from your net needle is secured to the bank line you will start forming the mesh. Begin where your needle is positioned at the right-hand side of your knots and work your way back to the first clove hitch. Hold your mesh gauge below the fifteen loops you created with your first set of knots. Bring your net needle cord behind the mesh gauge and through the first loop.

Setting Up the Mesh—Step Five

Pull the line the whole way through and tighten it against that mesh gauge. Then bring your line back up and around the back of your loop to make a knot. Work this way through all the loops until you get back to your first clove hitch. Hold the mesh gauge against your second set of loops and work your way to the end of the line, continuing to add to the loops until you reach your desired length.

Funnel Nets

Funnel nets should be placed with the opening on the upstream side of the stream. They can then be pegged in place, and you can create a further funnel with natural debris or bait them for larger animals like turtles. A funnel net is constructed like a gill net, except for the head rope. Here, circle and lash a natural material like a green branch as a hoop at the head of your funnel. In this trap the fish will swim in but cannot turn around in the back of the funnel.

Tumplines

The tumpline is a strap that extends around the load and is worn on the crown of the head. You bend slightly at the waist so that the weight is carried down the spine of the back and no tension is placed on your neck or shoulder muscles. Tumplines can be made from cordage, rope, or strapping, and are sometimes handwoven and ornately decorated. Most measure about 6′–12′ in length and have an approximate 2′ area in the center that is wider than the rest of the strap.

Two-Ply Cordage

Reverse-wrap, two-ply cordage can be made from an existing material such as a bank line to increase tensile strength or with natural fibers like barks twisted together.

Effective Trapping

Effective trapping requires some basic knowledge of animal behavioral patterns. You need to understand:

- What they eat
- Where they live
- Where they travel

Animal Diets

An animal's diet is another important factor in trapping because a baited trap is a hundred times more likely to catch an animal than a curiosity-type set that is not baited.

Animal Sign

Animal sign is the key to eliminating guesswork when setting your traps. Only trap where there is sign. Sign is anything the animal leaves as a trace that indicates it may have passed through the area. There are seven types of sign you need to know that will help you identify things like species, eating habits, and population numbers: tracks, scat, slough, remains, refuse, dens, and odor.

Animal Tracks

Examining tracks is the easiest way to identify the species. This can also help determine population numbers, frequency of travel in that area, and even preferred food in cases where you can tell that one animal has been trailing another.

Animal Scat

Scat left when an animal defecates can also help you identify species as well as what food source the animal is currently foraging.

Animal Remains

The dead body of an animal will not only provide possible resources such as bait and attractants for other traps, but it also may give some idea of what other animals are in the area.

Animal Slough

Slough is something from the animal's body left behind after it is gone. Examples include a strand of hair on a fence wire, a feather dropped while preening, or shed snakeskin.

*"The idea of wilderness needs no defense,
it needs only defenders."*

—EDWARD ABBEY

Animal Refuse

Refuse is the animal's garbage, which will help identify its species and its travel routes. For instance, a squirrel midden, or refuse heap, is its favorite spot and will be littered with shells from the nuts it has been eating. A beaver or muskrat leaves behind chewed trees and branches.

Animal Dens

A den is an animal's home. It can be a hole in the ground, in a bank, or in the hollow of a tree. The type of den is often a sure indicator of the species. You can usually set traps at the entrance or exit.

Animal Odor

Cat urine has a distinctive smell, as does rotten meat from a carnivore den where a fox might live. Obviously, you'll smell a skunk in the area, but other subtle smells can be identified as well.

Lower Food Chain Resources

Animals at the lower end of the food chain are what every other animal seeks for food. Around the water's edge this group includes frogs, crayfish, fish, as well as mussels and snails. Seeking these food items for yourself and then delegating a portion of them to the traps you build will enable you to catch more sizable prey items. If you are in an area that contains no water sources, you will need to microtrap in order to secure animals you can use as bait; for instance mice, rats, and chipmunks.

Gill or Stop Nets

Gill nets must be long enough to stretch from one side of a creek or small river to the other and deep enough to stretch from the top of the water to the bottom. This type of net is usually weighted with stones at the bottom and has some type of flotation device at the top. Drive fish into a gill net by walking downstream and chasing them into it. When they try to leave the net, their gills pass through the holes but their bodies cannot.

Seine Nets

A seine net is large with very small holes. It can be walked through a deeper water source and often has a long stick on each end that can be used to manipulate smaller fish to a place at the edge of the water where you can grab it.

Funnels

Funnels are traps woven from natural materials and employ two cones that fit together so that fish can swim in but cannot leave. By simply tying the funnels together, both facing the same direction, you make the trap easier to open. The same concept will work with a 2-liter bottle; cut off the top and turn it to the inside to trap smaller bait fish. This type of net is woven like a basket, and the outer piece has a hole in the bottom from which fish can swim into the larger cone where they will get trapped.

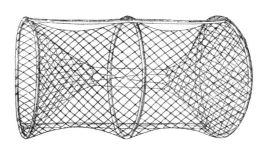

Fences

Fences are used to guide fish to a certain location in the water or animals such as turtles to a location on the water's edge. They can be built from any natural material including stones, sticks, or even logs. Fencing called a weir can be used to trap fish in a smaller area where they can be hunted with a bow or gig.

L7 Triggers

These are simple reverse notches that form a quick-release system. Employing L7 triggers in fishing involves using line and a trap together to actually set the hook after the animal runs with the bait. An L7 trigger is combined with a spring-pole device, allowing the line to be hand-cast off the bank with a baited hook. When the fish or turtle runs with the bait it dislodges the L7 trigger, which springs the pole and immediately jerks the line to set or lodge the hook in the throat of the prey.

Primitive Traps

Primitive traps are designed to accomplish at least one of three things: strangle, mangle, or dangle. Many of them use the common releases or triggering systems.

Windlass Machines (Kleptsy)

The windlass is used on this trap as a winding device. This creates spring-loaded tension to hold a killing device in place by a bait stick. When the bait stick is removed, it lets the windlass release, swinging the device under tension to kill the target prey. These traps involve a windlass machine that delivers a killing blow or deploys a spike or spear to impale the animal upon release of the trigger.

Suspended Deadfalls

Suspended deadfall traps involve a suspended deadfalling device above the ground that drops upon release. These can be combined with spikes or spear points for larger game.

Powered Snares

Snares involving a spring-loaded engine or a counterweight device can be very effective depending on the setup. They just need to lift the animal off the ground using noncable snares. Most snares will not catch the animal around the neck; more often than not, the snare will encircle the animal's body. Snare loops need to be set at a targeted diameter to ensure a proper catch.

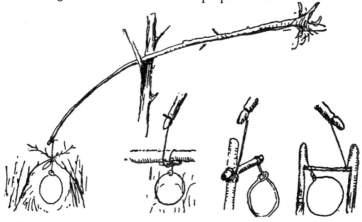

POLE FOR RABBIT SNARE AND VARIOUS WAYS OF SETTING THE NOOSE.

Free-Hanging Snares

Unpowered snares rely strictly on the animal's struggles to tighten and hold it in the trap. These are often the least effective traps when manufactured in a primitive fashion; however, cable snares in this configuration can be very effective.

Trapping Birds

All North American birds are edible and plentiful, which makes them a good choice for your table in a long-term outing. For catching birds, three traps work the best:

- Multiple ground snares
- Ojibwa bird traps
- Cage-style traps

*"I walked slowly to enjoy this freedom,
and when I came out of the mountains,
I saw the sky over the prairie, and I thought
that if heaven was real, I hoped it was a place
I never had to go, for this earth was
greater than any paradise."*

—DANIEL J. RICE, *THE UNPEOPLED SEASON*

Multiple Ground Snares

A simple stake in the ground surrounded by a small pile of ground debris can work with a group of small-diameter snares to create a network of ground snares. If you bait them with something on which the birds are feeding, such as small seeds, it is one of the most effective traps for small birds. They must be small—snares should be made from very fine line—and you need a lot of them, at least twenty- five snares with 2"–3" overlapping loops for a 2' square area.

Ojibwa Bird Trap–Step One

Get a pole tall enough for the bird to land on but not so tall that you won't be able to retrieve the bird after it's trapped. Sharpen it at both ends. Drill or carve a hole into the top of your pole, about 2" from the point. Place a second stick, about 4" long, into the hole. The diameter of this stick should be just a little bit less than the hole so that the stick rests in the hole rather than being tightly screwed into it. This stick will be the perch.

Ojibwa Bird Trap–Step Two

Select a piece of thin cordage about half the length of your pole; this is the snare. It is important that this cord is not too long or else your counterweight will rest on the ground instead of pulling tightly when the snare is activated. Tie a stop knot about one-third of the way into your cord. Use a clove hitch to create a loop in the other side of the knot on your cordage (the longer side). String the cordage through the hole on your pole.

Ojibwa Bird Trap–Step Three

Tie a rock that's about the size of the bird you intend to trap on the end opposite of the loop. Place your perch stick into the hole where you have strung the snare. Carefully lay the loop of your snare on the perch. This perch is the trigger stick, and when the bird lands on it the trap will drop the rock and activate the snare. The bird will instinctively grab the stick when it lands, which will ensure that its legs are inside the loop of your activated snare.

Cage-Style Traps—Step One

Before building a cage-style trap, you will need to prepare a series of sticks that are similar in diameter but get progressively shorter in length in order to build a cage similar to a pyramid. Make sure the sticks you select are fairly straight and about ½" in diameter. Cut two sticks for each of the following lengths: 12", 11", 10", 9", 8", 7", 6", and 5". Finally, cut six sticks about 4" long.

Cage-Style Traps—Step Two

Take the 12" sticks and place them parallel to each other, about a foot apart. Attach a length of cord between the two sticks about 1" from their top ends. Attach a length of cord, equal to the first, between the two sticks about 1" from their bottom ends. Flip one of the sticks over so that the cords cross each other to form an X.

Cage-Style Traps—Step Three

Push the 11" sticks under the cord, perpendicular to the 12" sticks, until they feel tight against the cord. The four sticks should now form a square. Now push the 10" sticks under the cord and over the 12" sticks until they feel tight. Push the 9" sticks under the cord and over the 11" sticks until they feel tight. Continue adding sticks under the cord, alternating sides like a log cabin until you get to the 4" sticks. Line these sticks in a row next to each other to create a secure roof on your cage.

"*Wilderness holds an original presence giving expression to that which we lack, the losses we long to recover, the absences we seek to fill. Wilderness revives the memory of unity. Through its protection we can find faith in our humanity.*"

—TERRY TEMPEST WILLIAMS,
RED: PASSION AND PATIENCE IN THE DESERT

Hunting

These days we put too much emphasis on the fastest-shooting bow and the longest-range rifles with expensive optics. Evolving and adapting to our environment is at the core of survival, so there are many benefits to the improvements in hunting practices. Even so, we have also lost many valuable skills such as stalking, closing distance, and tracking prey. These skills demonstrate true self-reliance.

Large Game versus Small Game

The question of whether to hunt large game such as deer or small game like rabbit depends on the situation. Logistically, large game takes large amounts of time and energy both to process and to preserve. Small game can be prepared easily and eaten on the spot if necessary. Large game is a much better option for long-term situations that involve a base camp with an operation for proper preserving.

Throwing Sticks

The throwing stick is one of the easiest improvised weapons to create and use effectively, even if you do not have a lot of practice. Its biggest convenience is that it can be carried on your belt so that it is out of the way and your hands are free until the second you need it. The reason that the throwing stick is so effective is that it rotates as you throw it so that even marginal shots can be successful. Think about how much easier it is to hit a squirrel with a shotgun compared to a rifle. It is all about surface area!

Throwing Stars

This weapon is a further innovation to the throwing stick. The throwing star uses two straight sticks with points on either end that are notched and lashed together to form an X or cross of sorts. This weapon relies on surface area and rotation and can be quite effective even on medium-sized animals such as raccoons. The main drawback to the throwing star is that it is cumbersome and cannot easily be stored, requiring you to hold it while you walk.

Spear Tips

Spears and gigs, easily improvised from natural material, work well as weapons. Spear tips can be made by fire-hardening wood or fashioning stone or pieces of glass into sharp points. Many knives now are designed to be used as spear points for emergencies. Commercial versions of gigs are available, but they can be easily fashioned from wood. Gigs work well for fishing and underwater use.

Slings

You can use any fabric, such as a bandanna or cordage, to make a sling that will allow you to launch a single stone at your prey. This is a frustrating weapon to master due to the limitations of working with one piece of ammunition at a time. It takes a lot of practice. The biggest advantage of using a sling is the abundance of ammunition; any semiround rock you can find will work.

Slingshots

The slingshot, in my opinion, is one of the most inexpensive and practical survival tools for short-term self-reliance. You can purchase commercial folding slingshots or make one yourself very cheaply, and ammunition is available along any creek bank. Slingshots are not difficult to master and fit easily into your daypack. To keep things light, you can even just carry the bands and improvise the frame with natural materials you find on the trail.

Bait

Most animals are easily attracted to bait not common to the area. For example, if black- or blue-colored berries are common in one area, bait a bird trap with red berries if you can find them. If hickory is the hardwood in an area you plan to trap squirrels, bait traps with walnuts instead.

Acorn Flour

Acorn flour was a staple food item for many native peoples throughout history and remains a major source of food for forest animals today. Its versatility makes it one of the eastern woodlands' best plant-based food resources. I tend to seek out white oak acorns because they have fewer tannins and taste less bitter. Tannins within the acorn can give it a very astringent taste. It is important that acorns are processed correctly so they have a gentler flavor.

Processing Acorn Flour–Step One

Crush the acorns with a rock or an axe. Then place the crushed acorns in a bowl of water; the shells will float and the meat will sink. Toss the shells. Drop the meat of the acorns in a clean batch of boiling water and let them cook until the water becomes brown. This discoloration is from the tannins. Place the acorn meat in another pot of boiling water and repeat the process. Make sure the water in the second pot is already boiling, because if the acorns come in contact with cold water, the process will undo itself.

Processing Acorn Flour–Step Two

You will likely need to move the acorn meat to a new pot of boiling water three or four times before the staining stops. When the majority of the tannins have been removed, the water will remain clear. If you don't have the necessary tools or setup, acorns can be leeched in running creek water by placing them in a cloth sack and leaving them in the creek for a week or so. However, the resulting flavor is not as reliable as what you get with the boiling method.

Processing Acorn Flour—Step Three

Once the meat is well soaked and clean you can use a stone to grind it into a meal for hot cereal, use it as a bread ingredient, or dry it out and store it for later use. If you decide to save the acorn flour for later, plan to soak it in water before you use it to rehydrate it to its mushy state.

Cattail Flour

Collect a good bucketful of cattail roots. Once you have washed and thoroughly peeled them, place them in a bucket of clean water. Break up the roots, which causes the flour to separate from the fibers. Continue until you have separated all the fibers in the roots. As you work, the flour will settle at the bottom of the bucket. Pour out the excess water and dump the remaining mush on a flat surface where it can dry in the sun. Once the flour is completely dry, store it in a cool, dry place away from insects.

Hickory Nuts

Hickory nuts are delicious and especially valuable because their shells efficiently lock out moisture and insects, so they keep for a very long time. Turn the nut so that it is lying sideways and the sharp, raised edge is on top. (Basically, turn it to the spot where it wobbles and will not stand on its own.) Then strike the seam in a spot about one-third of the way from the base of the stem. If you follow these steps, you should easily pop the nut into three pieces every time with plenty of exposed meat for the picking.

Pine Nuts

All pine nut seeds are edible, so you do not need to worry about identifying different species. Some have larger seeds than others, and even though you can eat them green, the older ones taste better. Look for cones that are turning brown but have not yet opened. Arrange them around a fire, and the warmth will force them open so that you can collect the seeds. Just be careful of mildew, which is the enemy of any seed. Keeping them dry is the key.

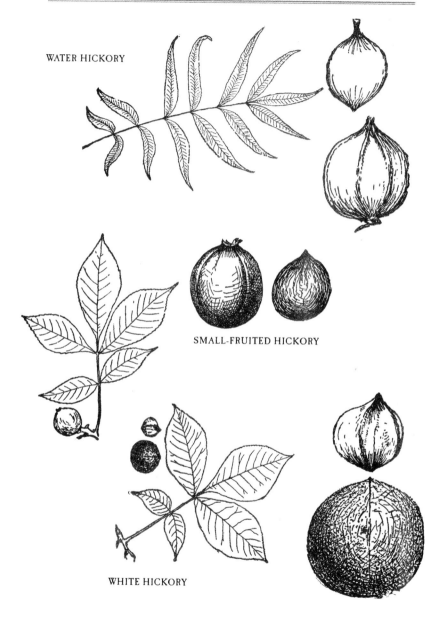

WATER HICKORY

SMALL-FRUITED HICKORY

WHITE HICKORY

*"There are no words that can tell
the hidden spirit of the wilderness,
that can reveal its mystery, its melancholy,
and its charm."*

—THEODORE ROOSEVELT

Walnuts

If possible, collect walnuts before they fall from the tree and then store them until they turn black. Remove the outer skins from the shells when they turn black and use them for dyes and medicines. Once you have the nut shells, you can then break them open and eat the meat inside. Walnuts do not store in the shell as well as hickory nuts. If you decide to save them for future use, dry them before storing. Leave them in the shell and crack it open just before eating.

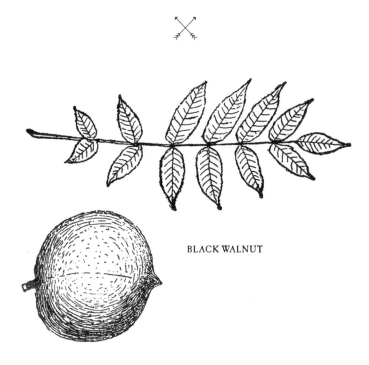

BLACK WALNUT

Foraging for Berries

Make certain you can identify any berries before eating them. When in doubt, do not eat! When looking for berries, scan the area from ground level to eye level. Look for low fruit trees and bushes. A lot of species are creepers, so scan the ground very well. Remember that berry plants are biologically constructed to protect themselves from birds. So they are often hiding under greenery or surrounded with thorns. Keep a close eye out for poison ivy, too.

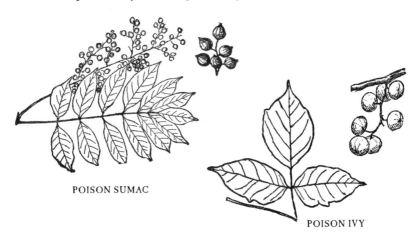

POISON SUMAC

POISON IVY

Bulbs As Food

Bulbs can be stored in a cool, dry place for a whole season. There are some great plants with edible bulbs, such as wild garlic or onion garlic, in the woodlands. Ramps and leeks also contain edible and delicious bulbs.

Fruit Leather

First mash and grind the fruit into a purée and pick out the seeds. Spread the purée over a flat surface, like a rock or cutting board that is about 1/8" thick. Leave it in the sun to dry for a few hours. You will know the fruit leather is ready by the glossy look the purée will get when it dries. Store it in a cool place where it will be safe from bugs and moisture. You can eat it as it is, rehydrate it to make drinks, or use it as an additive for recipes such as bread and cereal.

Edible Roots and Tubers

Cattail contains an edible, starchy tuber that can be eaten as well as stored dry. Arrowhead is another water plant with an edible tuber that has high starch content. Burdock contains a large taproot similar to the potato and can be easily stored for later use if kept dry. Dandelion root makes a good drink or coffee substitute. Yellow nut grass is another edible root plant native around areas of water where cattails and arrowhead are found.

Maple Syrup

Once you've collected maple sap, pour it into a cooking pot until the pot is about three-quarters full and boil to evaporate all of the water content. This will take several hours of constant boiling. Keep an eye on the color. The syrup should gradually turn gold and then darken until it becomes the mahogany shade of maple syrup. Once the syrup is complete, strain the liquid to get rid of any particles that may have fallen into the concoction during the long boiling process. Pour into glass jars or plastic containers and store in a cool place.

Maple Sugar

You can further process maple syrup into a delicious sweetener called maple sugar. Bring maple syrup to a boil and skim off the air bubbles as they rise. Reduce the heat a little if it starts to boil over the sides of the pot. When the air bubbles stop appearing, remove the liquid from the heat and transfer it to a wooden bowl. Stir for at least

5 minutes to remove any remaining moisture and then let it stand until it turns hard. This hard material can be ground into sugar and stored in a cool place.

Salt Drying Meat

Drying meat involves pulling moisture from the meat at a slow rate so that the outside of the meat does not dry first. Moisture is the enemy in meat preservation because it allows bacteria to grow. With this understanding, two environmental conditions are necessary for properly drying meat:

- A humidity level of about 30 percent or less
- A few straight days with an even temperature where there is little fluctuation from day to night

Wild Spices/Herbs

Most wild herbs can be air-dried for later use. You can grind these dried spices into flavorings for food and teas. A few of my favorites are mustard seed, garlic mustard, mint, shepherd's purse, and dock seeds.

Salt Solution for Drying Meat and Fish

- 1 gallon water
- 20 ounces salt

Stir the salt into the water until dissolved. Dip the strips into the salt solution right before hanging. Suspend the meat strips vertically by the thickest end. Attach them to a line with loops of cordage of a small diameter if possible. Dried meat can then be stored in a breathable bag. You can eat it just as it is or rehydrate right before use.

Sun Drying Fish

Remove the heads and guts and then split the fish right at the spine. Now you should have two pieces, side by side with the skin on top of each. From here, cut the fish into several equal chunks. Fish will generally dry more quickly than red meat, but still dip the strips into the salt solution. Dry the fish strips on racks, which you can easily fashion with two tripods and a cross stick.

Jerky

You can make jerky by adding a good salt solution and some spice to the meat, which is then dried over a low-heat fire of about 120°F. Cut the meat into lean, thin strips. If done properly, a pound of meat will reduce to about 4 ounces in weight. When finished, the meat should crack when bent but not snap in half. It should be dry and not moist or greasy.

Cold Smoking

The cold-smoking process is similar to making jerky in that you are cutting meat into thin strips, salting, and drying with an elevated temperature. Here, meat is dried at a temperature that is lower than what you use for jerky—about 85°F. You want a fire with lots of smoke to add flavor (and deter bugs). This method takes 12–24 hours in most cases.

Cold Hanging

In the winter, if the temperatures linger around freezing for a few days, meat can safely hang to dry. The cold temperatures ensure that bacteria do not develop. In this process, the meat does not need to be deboned and cut into strips, but the animal must be completely gutted and opened with a cross stick in the breast so that the carcass stays open while it dries.

Extracting Salt

Salt can be a major concern for the longer term, but some plants contain enough salt that you can actually extract by boiling them. Hickory is one tree that will provide salt if the roots are cut and boiled. Once the water has completely boiled away there will be a black substance left that will be salt. Animal blood is another resource rich in salt and many other nutrients. Note that when you extract salt from hickory you will actually be rendering mineral salt. That means it takes a lot to make very little.

Natural Dyes

Many fruits and plants also produce natural dyes. Raspberry will make red, goldenrod is deep brown, pokeberries make a purple dye, bloodroot is orange to reddish. Dyes made from berries can be soaked in a hot fixative of salt water, while most plants will require vinegar for fixing.

Making Natural Ink

To make ink, macerate pokeberries (poisonous) in a pan or container. Add enough water to cover the material, which should equal about 1 cup in total, and slowly bring to a boil. Remove from heat, add 1 teaspoon salt, and, if available, 1 teaspoon vinegar, and simmer 15 minutes. Mix well to dilute the ingredients and strain the liquid into a storage container or bottle that can be sealed. Any large feather can be fashioned into a pen.

Vinegar in the Wilderness

Anything that will ferment will eventually turn to vinegar. If you need vinegar as a fixative for something, a simple punch made from wild berries can be covered until it ferments (turns to alcohol), then leave it in the open air for a couple of weeks and it will turn to vinegar.

Casing

Casing is a process of removing the hide from the carcass that works well for smaller animals. To case an animal, you remove the skin from one side of the carcass to the other in one continuous piece, almost like a tube.

Large Hides

Large hides from animals such as deer can be split and sewn together for more involved projects like clothing and shelter resources.

Fleshing and Drying

Fleshing refers to the process of removing all the meat and membrane from the gut side of the hide. Fleshing beams can be easily constructed with a large log and a homemade tripod. Find a log about 8" in diameter and strip off all of the bark. Use the tripod to elevate one end of the log. If you want to use a hide without hair, to make leather for example, then either pull off the hair during the fleshing process or soak the hide in ash water for a couple of days and then strip the hair.

Splitting

The most effective way to remove a hide from a large carcass is to split the hide. In this process, you hang an animal upside down and cut the belly to open the hide with the gut side out. From here you cut across both inside back legs between the anus and vent or penis, and from there you basically strip the hide down off the carcass similar to the way you would pull off a shirt.

Rawhide

When the hide has been fleshed and dried and the hair has been removed you will have rawhide. Rawhide can be used for many things.

Bark Tanning

First, make bark liquor by boiling large amounts of bark (such as walnut or white oak) in three batches of varying concentrations. The first batch should be made very strong; the third batch should be the weakest. Soak the hide in the first batch for a couple of weeks. During the first few days stir it often and then several times a day after that. The hide is then stored in the second batch for 4 weeks with the same stirring frequency. The hide is stored in the last batch for up to 12 weeks. After, you still need to oil the hide, dry it, break down the fibers, and waterproof.

Pot Scrubbers

If you need a simple pot scrubber, take some broom sedge, fold it in half, and wrap it one time as you would a besom at a point about ½" from the top. Cut it to about 3" total and you will have a great pot and pan cleaner.

Water Containers

Water containers should be of such material that you can use them to carry water over a distance and also as cooking vessels at camp. Metal tends to be the best option because it can be placed right into the fire. You can also fold over a simple piece of canvas, sew it, and create a container to carry several gallons of water over a distance. You can also carve and burn containers out of wood.

Lockstitch

Whatever the length of the lockstitch needed, you will require about
twice that length of thread. Once the first hole is punched, pull half
of the thread to the opposite side of the fabric. With the remaining
length of thread, make a loop near the hole through which you've
just passed your needle. Now pass the needle along with the thread
through the loop and pull tight. Repeat this process. To finish,
secure your stitching with a double stitch and then a few stitches
in the reverse direction.

Running Stitch

A running stitch can be used to repair seams or hems on thinner
fabrics like cotton. A running stitch is a simple in-and-out stitch
evenly spaced in a line going through one side and coming back
through the other with no locking thread. You can use this stitch
to connect materials like sleeves to a shirt.

Whipstitch

A whipstitch is used for seams as well, and actually goes around the fabric fold in a spiral pattern, rolling the material as the stitch line progresses to create a welt. This is a good stitch for connecting two separate pieces as well as finishing things like tarp edges and jacket seams. It is suitable for very strong material, even on hide materials, brain-tanned hides, and moccasins.

Saddle Stitch

A saddle stitch is used mainly for heavy materials such as leather. It involves two needles, one on each end of the thread or cord, that pass through the same hole in opposite directions to create a locked running stitch. When using this type of stitch you will want to use a non-awl-type needle and pre-punched holes so that the thread passes through the fabric easily without breaking.

Felling Axe

A felling axe is a little bit larger than the usual model. At minimum, this axe has about a 3-pound head weight and has a 36"-long handle. This is the best tool for harvesting larger pieces of lumber.

Broad Axe

The broad axe is the best tool for removing the last bit of material from the facing side of a log. It only needs to be sharpened on one side so that it can be used like a chisel. Sizes vary—some broad axes have smaller head weights and short handles, while others are very large. My suggestion is to carry a smaller broad axe and complement it with a larger adze.

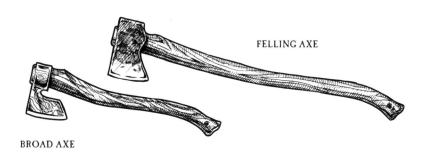

FELLING AXE

BROAD AXE

Adze

Adzes are used for flattening the sides of
logs and truing the flats. An adze can be
used in place of the broad axe in some
cases because it works on similar logs but is more
versatile. A curved adze can be used for many large-
scale carving tasks such as hollowing out large basins
or making dugouts.

Froe

A froe is a long, flat blade with an upright handle. This tool is used
to split lumber along the grain to create flat pieces of wood such as
boards and shingles.

Replacing Tool Handles

Hickory is the preferred wood for straight tool handles. For bent handles, ash is the better wood. For shorter handles or for mauls, maple is a good choice. Handles are generally made from green sapwood. Heartwood within the handle may cause warping during the drying and curing process. Some shrinking will occur also, so make handles a little oversized in width. It takes several weeks for green wood to fully dry before the handle can be finally shaped and helved to the tool.

Bucksaw

A large bucksaw or bow saw is used to break down longer logs when creating shingles and smaller lumber boards. The bucksaw is great for breaking down firewood as well. I recommend the 36" bucksaw.

Wood Density

If you are not sure about the wood density or hardness of the wood you are working, place it in water. Softwoods will float high in the water, while some hardwoods will actually sink.

Log Dogs

Log dogs are metal-forged U brackets. The sides of the U are right angles, which makes them look square in shape. These log dogs are used to secure a log so that it does not roll while you are working on it. Notch two smaller logs with V cuts and place the working log right in their cutouts. These V cuts will cradle the log. Then pound in the log dogs with a maul so that one end of the dog is in the working log and one end is in the cradle log at an angle.

Processing a Tree to Create Lumber–Step One

Once you have selected a log for your project, lay it on the ground in your workspace, cradled by two smaller logs with log dogs attached to each end. Now you will need to hew the log, or square it. Start by removing a line of bark from end to end across the face so that you end up with the thickness that you need. Picture the front of the log as the top of a stump when you are squaring it. This gives you an idea of how deep to make that first cut.

Processing a Tree to Create Lumber–Step Two

Clear the bark and pop a line, using string wiped with charcoal, from end to end. This will make your cut line clear and visible. Start by making a series of V cuts with your axe about 2' apart down that cut line on the face of the log. These V cuts should stretch the entire length of the log. Then remove these 2' pieces with your axe.

Processing a Tree to Create Lumber–Step Three

When the job is completed, you should have a rough flat surface on one side of the log. Remove the dogs and turn the log over so that the other side is facing up and reattach the dogs. You can use an adze to square the surface. Repeat this process three more times on the log and you will have one piece of square timber.

Image Credits